spirit of garbo

spirit
of garbo
moon
laramie

martin firrell company
MODERN ESOTERICA

First published in 2018 by Martin Firrell Company Ltd
10 Queen Street Place, London EC4R 1AG, United Kingdom.

ISBN 978-0-9931786-7-2

Text is set in Baskerville, 12pt on 17pt.

Baskerville is a serif typeface designed in 1754 by John Baskerville (1706–1775) in Birmingham, England. Compared to earlier typeface designs, Baskerville increased the contrast between thick and thin strokes. Serifs were made sharper and more tapered, and the axis of rounded letters was placed in a more vertical position. The curved strokes were made more circular in shape, and the characters became more regular.

Baskerville is categorized as a transitional typeface between classical typefaces and high contrast modern faces. Of his own typeface, John Baskerville wrote, 'Having been an early admirer of the beauty of letters, I became insensibly desirous of contributing to the perfection of them. I formed to myself ideas of greater accuracy than had yet appeared, and had endeavoured to produce a set of types according to what I conceived to be their true proportion.'

Contents

11:   *There is a freedom which is mine.*

19:   *I don't believe in half measures.*
       I want to live honestly.

31:   *What about the enemy's god?*

43:   *I know some very nice people in the gutter.*

53:   *I shall always dress for dinner.*

63:   *I have nothing to reproach myself with and I am*
       indifferent to public opinion.

73:   *I've heard so much about you I know we will*
       be friends.

83:   *Lonely? I've never been so contented in my life.*

93:   *You have a queer way of looking at things.*

107:   *Not to think, only to live, only to feel.*

115:   *Happiness you cannot imagine. Happiness you*
       must feel.

123:   *She is rather a crazy mystic Swede.*

145:   *What's important is that whenever you meet your*
       fellow man, you're kind and you're decent.

155:   *I want to cultivate the art of peace, the art of life.*

163:   *I am afraid of nothing, except being bored.*

175: Filmography

183: Notes

185: Bibliography

187: Index

193: About the author

A note to the reader

Spirit of Garbo is not a biography in the conventional sense: it is not a chronological retelling of the events of Greta Garbo's life.

Instead it traces the arc of her spiritual development, describing her rapid self-actualisation and her interest in esotericism.

In non-chronological order, it cites those incidents in her life that best illustrate her spiritual growth.

There is a freedom which is mine.

GARBO IN QUEEN CHRISTINA
METRO-GOLDWYN-MAYER 1933

Future generations may envy us, for we saw her in her own time. They, too, will wonder at the mysteries surrounding her - those mysteries that were conjured up on the day when the forgotten genius Mauritz Stiller, out of the misery of his haunted childhood, imagined he saw someone - goddess or snow maiden - so beautiful that she could scarcely be believed, and called her Garbo.[1]

Greta Garbo was born Greta Lovisa Gustafsson on 18 September 1905 in Södermalm, a poor, run-down district in Stockholm, Sweden. Her parents were Karl Alfred Gustafsson and Anna Lovisa Karlsson. When the couple married hurriedly on 8 May 1898, Anna was already pregnant with their first child, Greta's elder brother Sven. To have a child out of wedlock was socially unacceptable and the need to protect their reputations had compelled the couple into a hasty union. Greta also had an elder sister, Alva Maria, born two years before her in September 1903. Her father Karl Alfred supported the family through a variety of low paid jobs. He suffered from poor health which prevented him from earning a regular income and the young Greta was a frequent visitor to the local soup kitchens.

Even as a young child, Greta dreamed of being an actress. From her penurious beginnings, she became one of the most celebrated artists in the history of cinema. Between 1926 and 1942, she made a total of twenty-six films, earning Metro-Goldwyn-Mayer unprecedented profits and making her Hollywood's most valuable asset. She was admired by women and men alike. She was an enigma, the object of universal affection, the world's first global celebrity. Her fame and notoriety remain unrivalled to this day. After her death in 1990, buyers were prepared to pay vastly inflated sums at the sale of her private art collection just to own something that had once belonged to the great Greta Garbo.

Her rise to fame, although meteoric, did not begin smoothly. Garbo arrived in America with her mentor, the Finnish-Swedish film director Mauritz Stiller, in July 1925. On her arrival, studio executives considered her unremarkable. The journalist Dorothy Woodridge observed of Garbo, 'Her shoes were run down at the heels. Her stockings were silk, but in one was a well-defined run. As a sartorial masterpiece she was a total loss.'[2] What Dorothy Woodridge had failed to understand was Garbo's fundamental indifference to superficial appearances. Despite that indifference, within a few short years Garbo would become Hollywood's most admired leading actress.

In the silent movie *The Mysterious Lady* (Metro-Goldwyn-Mayer, 1928), Garbo plays the seductive Russian spy Tania Fedorova. She lights up the screen from the moment Captain Karl von Raden (Conrad Nagel) encounters her at the Opera House in Vienna. Greta Garbo had somehow transformed herself. Her screen presence had attained an ineffable luminescence and power but her transformation remains shrouded in mystery still. Orson Welles, interviewed by Michael Parkinson in 1974, describes visiting the Swedish Film Institute in Stockholm where he was shown an advertisement for bread from the archives. It featured Garbo, then an unknown actress, in one of her earliest roles. Welles is struck by the mystery of her transformation: 'There was this great galumphing Swedish cow having a picnic. There was nothing to show you that you were looking at the most divine creature that would ever be on the screen, and two years later she was Greta Garbo. I have no explanation whatsoever for that.' The answer can be found, perhaps, in Garbo's close association with Mauritz Stiller. Born in 1883 in Russian occupied Finland, Stiller fled to Stockholm in 1904 to escape conscription. After a brief period working in theatre, he landed a job as a director for Charles Magnusson's Svenska Bio film company. He would make his one and only film with Garbo, *Gösta Berlings Saga* (AB Svensk Filmindustri), in 1924 but he would continue to mentor her for many years. During their time together, Stiller tutored Garbo tirelessly, helping her fashion her inner and outer selves into an integrated whole. Garbo's film career enabled her to support her family financially as well as bringing her into contact with many leading artists and intellectuals of the day. The arc of her life and her development as an artist can be seen to reveal an inner spirit progressing towards what modern psychology has come to describe as 'self-actualisation'.

The concept of self-actualisation was introduced by the German neurologist Kurt Goldstein and developed further by the American psychologist Abraham Maslow. Maslow first met Goldstein at Brandeis University and became greatly influenced by his ideas. Maslow was particularly fascinated by the concept of self-actualisation, so much so that self-actualisation became the ultimate goal of his now famous Hierarchy of Needs. Maslow believed self-actualisation represented the pinnacle of an individual's personal growth. He viewed it as the 'single ultimate value for mankind, a far goal toward which all men strive'. For Maslow, self-actualisation meant 'realising the potentialities of the person, that is to say, becoming fully human, everything that the person can become'.[3] Maslow noted that individuals who were self-actualised felt a deeper consciousness, an inner harmony, that enabled them to move more lightly through the world. They encountered periods of intense feeling that Maslow described as peak experiences - moments of rapture when the individual feels a sense of oneness with the universe. Self-actualised people regularly have mystical and expansive instances of peak experience.

Maslow's studies were considered groundbreaking because he worked with subjects who were psychologically healthy rather than those with deep-rooted psychological problems. Through his observations, he was able to define a set of qualities characteristic of the self-actualised individual. Both the inner and outer lives of self-actualised people are consistent, integrated and authentic. Self-actualised people avoid knee-jerk or reactionary responses to conflict situations. They see no need to label other people or make generalisations about them. They are comfortable with who they are. They recognise their own worth. They recognise the value in other human beings. They are unperturbed by silence or solitude. They are independent thinkers. They are able to live fully in the present moment. They have more peak experiences more often. They see their own interconnectedness with the rest of the cosmos. They have a well-developed sense of compassion. Their lives have meaning and purpose. They live their lives free from fear. Maslow expressed the view that there were extremely few self-actualised people in the world.

Greta Garbo declined to adopt the lifestyle expected of someone in her position in Hollywood. She relished the craft of acting and wanted to make films of artistic merit. But she didn't feel the same way about the public relations circus that attends the film-making business. She regarded publicity as inherently substanceless and an unnecessary distraction. Like all self-actualised people, Garbo danced to her own tune. She revealed herself to be a spiritual seeker interested in life's essential meaning and the truths of the Ageless Wisdom. She developed close relationships with others who travelled a similar path. Authenticity of feeling and being mattered far more to her than the outer trappings of fame or glamour.

I don't believe in half measures. I want to live honestly.

GARBO IN THE SINGLE STANDARD
METRO-GOLDWYN-MAYER 1929

Both the inner and outer lives of self-actualised people are consistent, integrated and authentic.

There are certain people who do not conform to social norms or other people's expectations. They are autonomous freethinkers who set their own parameters. People with these qualities are precisely the kind of people Maslow described as self-actualised. Self-actualised people are authentic and self-integrated. In existentialist philosophy 'authenticity' is defined as the ability to be true to one's own spirit. Self-integration is the consolidation of one's personal characteristics into a unified and harmonious whole. The self-actualised aspire to the realisation of personal truth, free from internal conflict. What they feel on the inside aligns with how they live on the outside.

In December 1923, Greta Gustafsson changed her name to Greta Garbo. In Italian and Spanish the word 'garbo' means 'gracefulness'. 'Garbo' was a name that better reflected the person Greta Gustafsson wanted to be. For the 'great galumphing Swedish cow' described by Orson Welles, it was an act of aspiration, requiring courage and determination. As a stage name, it was modern, elegant and international, accessible to audiences anywhere in the world. By taking a new name, Garbo had begun emphatically to steer her own course. In his role as friend and mentor, Mauritz Stiller counselled Garbo to celebrate her individuality. She should never seek to imitate her contemporaries, he advised. She was uniquely Garbo. The writer and conservationist Louis Bromfield believed her success as an actress came down to one thing: her consummate authenticity. Bromfield said of Garbo that she had learned to be wholly and fully herself. On camera, this inner authenticity allowed her to deliver a resolutely coherent performance. She was able to convey emotions with the most fleeting of expressions. This was why her cameraman William Daniels so often chose to film her in close up. Her performances had a transcending, mesmeric quality of which the viewer never tired. Dorothy Herzog of the *New York Mirror* described her ability to move 'Cleopatra-like' with 'alluring mouth and volcanic, slumbrous eyes'. On set, Garbo's pragmatic and genuine nature meant that she quickly earned the affection of film crews. William Daniels felt that her most ardent fans were the people she worked with every day.

Tennessee Williams wanted Garbo for the part of Blanche DuBois in the film version of *A Streetcar Named Desire*. In Williams' play Blanche DuBois isn't interested in the truth. She prefers to talk about what 'ought to be the truth'. Garbo declined the role. She confided to her friend, the photographer Cecil Beaton, that she was far too honest and clear cut to play someone as mendacious as DuBois. Garbo was attracted to playing women of a very different kind. In Tolstoy's novel *Anna Karenina,* Anna reveals herself to be the most integrated character in the book as she responds fully and faithfully to her emotions. The strength of her conviction enables her to break away from societal conventions and sacrifice social position for love. Garbo performed the role twice for Metro-Goldwyn-Mayer, once in the 1927 silent film released as *Love*, directed by Edmund

Goulding, and again in 1935's *Anna Karenina*, directed by Clarence Brown. During one of the pivotal scenes in *Anna Karenina*, Anna's husband warns her that her friendship with Count Vronsky is attracting gossip. His reason for warning her, he claims, is because he loves her. She suggests in reply, that it is his career and maintaining appearances that he loves, not her.

In *Queen Christina* (Metro-Goldwyn-Mayer, 1933) the 17th-century Swedish monarch refuses to marry the Spanish King, abdicating to be with the man she truly loves. Garbo was drawn to the character's self-possession and willingness to act in accordance with her personal truth. Garbo portrayed Queen Christina in a landmark performance opposite her close friend and sometime beau John Gilbert. (Garbo and Gilbert's intensely-felt and wildly volatile relationship became the talk of the gossip columns, even prompting a poem in *Photoplay* entitled 'Off Again, On Again, Greta and John Again'.) Queen Christina's strength of character echoed Garbo's own. In a 1959 interview for *This Week*, the Greek shipping magnate Aristotle Onassis described Garbo as utterly natural, direct and honest.

From the very beginning, Garbo was interested in the process of making films rather than the celebrity that came with success in her chosen profession. This explains her often ambiguous relationship with the American film industry. She wanted her films to be artistically significant and failed to see how appearing on the red carpet at a film's premiere would contribute to its creative merit. In order to remain authentic in Hollywood, she resolved to do things on her own terms. In her original screen test Garbo was criticised by studio executives for not being sufficiently 'glamorous'. In response, she said this was who she was. The studio could take it or leave it.

The director Ernst Lubitsch was famous for his refined comedies of manners, earning himself an Honorary Academy Award in 1946 for his contribution to film. He directed Garbo in her first comedy, *Ninotchka* (Metro-Goldwyn-Mayer, 1939). Lubitsch noted that many actors were obsessed with their own reflection, but not Garbo. She would only look in the mirror when he told her to do so.

At a party on the Onassis yacht in 1955, the super rich were gathered, displaying their wealth conspicuously in the form of French haute couture and priceless jewellery. Garbo arrived in a drab green satin dress and a pair of sandals, wearing no jewellery at all. Conversation gave way to startled silence as the assembled guests realised who had entered the party and how plainly dressed she was. To them outward appearance meant everything. To Garbo it meant little or nothing. The journalist Sven Broman befriended Garbo in her old age. He detected no bitterness in her about ageing and at no point did she try to appear younger than she was. Cosmetic surgery was something for the rest of Hollywood, perhaps, but not for her. A doctor once advised her to be glad she was in the second half of her life: youth was wasted on the young. She agreed. The attempt to maintain a false semblance of youth simply held no interest for her. She had no appetite for falsifying her words either. She was always frank about her attitude to Hollywood's publicity machine and her candour caused endless headaches for Howard Dietz, head of public relations at Metro-Goldwyn-Mayer. He attempted to rein her in by suggesting he would send a chaperone to every interview she gave. Garbo told him if she couldn't speak freely she wouldn't speak at all. True to her word, she didn't give another formal interview for over forty years.

Garbo was drawn to playing women with strong convictions. In *A Woman Of Affairs* (Metro-Goldwyn-Mayer, 1928), she plays Diana Merrick, an English socialite whose husband David (Johnny Mack Brown) commits suicide. The real reason for his suicide is financial: David realises he is going to be tried for embezzlement so he kills himself to protect his wife from the scandal. Groundless rumours abound that it was Diana who drove him to take his own life. Despite the damage to her own reputation, Diana remains silent about the true reason so protecting the memory of her late husband as an honest man. In widowhood, she embarks on a free-spirited odyssey, travelling across Europe and seeking solace in the arms of a string of lovers. The one constant person in her life has been her childhood sweetheart Neville (John Gilbert). Even though they can never be together (Neville is now happily married) she tells him she has only ever said 'I love you' to one man - and he is that man. In *Anna Christie* (Metro-Goldwyn-Mayer, 1930), Garbo's Anna feels compelled to tell her admirer Matt

(Charles Bickford) that she has had many previous lovers. She risks losing him by revealing the truth. He is so struck by her sincerity he realises he truly loves her regardless of her past. As the eponymous spy and femme fatale, Garbo prepares to face the firing squad at the end of *Mata Hari* (Metro-Goldwyn-Mayer, 1931). She asks her advocate to do one last thing for her - to tell her lover Alexis (Ramon Novarro) that no matter what he hears, her love for him was 'honest'. In *Two-Faced Woman* (Metro-Goldwyn-Mayer, 1941), she accuses her husband Larry (Melvyn Douglas) of lying to her. He suggests that duplicity is acceptable. He tells her that in many ways life is a half truth and a compromise. 'Not my life,' Garbo replies.

On those rare occasions when her characters are forced to lie, they are always motivated by consideration for others. In *A Woman Of Affairs,* Garbo's character is reunited with her true love, Neville, but spares Neville's wife Constance by telling her, untruthfully, that there are no romantic feelings between them. She understands that the truth would destroy Neville's marriage. Similarly in *Torrent* (Metro-Goldwyn-Mayer, 1923), she refuses to run away with her old flame Rafael (Ricardo Cortez), insisting she could never rob his wife of her husband or his children of their father.

Money held little fascination for Garbo. In *Inspiration* (Metro-Goldwyn-Mayer, 1931) Marta, the housekeeper, tells Garbo that rich men do not grow on trees. She replies that she has no need of rich men. Garbo's contract required the studio to pay her a weekly surcharge of $10,000 if shooting ran over schedule. When production delays triggered this clause in her contract, she returned the money. On completion of her last film, Metro-Goldwyn-Mayer was obliged to pay her an additional $250,000 whether she made another film or not. There was no love lost between Garbo and studio head Louis B. Mayer, and she might easily have held Mayer to the contract, but instead she released the studio from its obligations entirely.

Garbo favoured flat shoes both on and off set. Flat shoes were practical, high heels were not. In the interests of comfort, she often wore carpet slippers when shooting, only taking them off if her feet were going to be in shot. The director Billy Wilder once remarked that Garbo was as out of place in Hollywood as Sibelius would have been writing movie scores for Warner Brothers. The German actor and director Gustav von Seyffertitz described Garbo as unusually unassuming with no apparent need to be the centre of attention. The British playwright Kenneth Jupp remarked that Garbo's true genius was as a listener. In conversation, she genuinely listened to the other speaker. He believed her power as an actress came from this ability to concentrate actively. When playing a scene she was capable of being fully present in the moment. Her mind was never elsewhere. Film-making itself can be regarded as the manipulation of time, capturing and storing an eternal present for future audiences to experience. But there was no disconnection or separation between Garbo and the present moment. As she grew older, she chose to spend more and more time taking meditative walks in the Swiss Alps. Garbo was evidently a child of nature. She enjoyed the tranquil simplicity of the moment. Film publicist Hubert Voight described her as a child of the sun, shining with life. This underlying vitality of spirit is captured in a brief exchange in *Two-Faced Woman*. Constance Bennet, as Griselda Vaughn, asks Garbo, what is her forte? Garbo replies, 'Life!'

Garbo's inner wholeness, and the surety it brought her, enabled her to weather the pressures of life under constant media scrutiny. Besieged by reporters in Rome in 1949, she announced, 'I want to be alone!' in a humorous reference to the quote most famously attributed to her. In *Ninotchka*, Garbo tells Count Léon's butler, 'Go to bed little father. We want to be alone!' Both on and off screen, she used the phrase for its full comic effect. When told that the author Norman Mailer had described her as an intelligent woman of beauty and greatness, she said the illusion would certainly be destroyed if they ever met so now she had better avoid him for the rest of her life. Garbo laughed at the idea of herself as the great movie star. Her true interest lay in exploring her abilities as an actor and her celebrity was an unfortunate side effect. Ernst Lubitsch observed that Garbo had a smile for every occasion. Each one was beautiful and unique. During the making of *Ninotchka*, the supposedly saturnine Garbo sat with Lubitsch in his office laughing continuously for a full ten minutes. Garbo was nominated for an Oscar as best actress for her role in the film. She lost to Vivien Leigh for her portrayal of Scarlett O'Hara in *Gone*

With the Wind. Leigh was elated to have beaten Hollywood's biggest box office star. Garbo was typically unfazed, declining to attend the ceremony in true Garbo style. Garbo had sufficient inner conviction to make her own way in the world. She paid no attention to the expectations of Hollywood's ruling elite - the studio executives. In many of the films they financed, she was able to play characters with an authenticity she shared. As Mata Hari, Garbo declares that she is her own person. As Queen Christina, she speaks of a freedom which belongs to her that nobody can take away. It was precisely convictions of this kind that caused so much consternation among studio executives. But in Hollywood it was also what made her unique.

What about the enemy's god?

GARBO IN QUEEN CHRISTINA
METRO-GOLDWYN-MAYER 1933

Self-actualised people avoid knee-jerk or reactionary responses to conflict situations.

Garbo starred opposite her fellow swede Nils Asther twice, once in *Wild Orchids* and once in *The Single Standard* (both Metro-Goldwyn-Mayer, 1929). On set one day, Asther asked her why she looked so sad. Garbo told him, 'I had an awful row with God this morning.' A sense of personal connection to the divine can be both complex and problematic. In *The Key to Theosophy*, the Russian occultist and mystic Helena Blavatsky discusses how easily a sense of fellowship with God can be exploited and abused. Blavatsky points to the paradox of two opposing armies both claiming to have God on their side. As she puts it, a general will invoke God to ask for 'help to cut his enemies' throats'. All too often, opposing groups justify atrocities by claiming their actions are vindicated by God or by the demands of justice. This is, of course, a perversion. Justice cannot be used to vindicate injustice, nobody has exclusive access to the divine. Garbo recognised that all human beings are essentially part of a universal brotherhood. This idea of universality was explored through many of the characters she played. Queen Christina of Sweden was a liberal monarch who fostered religious tolerance. She took the counsel of French Catholic freethinkers. This pitted her against Sweden's close-minded Lutherans. In the role of Queen Christina, Garbo is told that her countrymen are fighting a war for their particular faith and for their god. Garbo asks, 'What about the enemy's god?' Garbo's Christina sees that there is both a core legitimacy and a unity between different peoples and different faiths. Christina recognises that to reject conflict and embrace interconnectedness must be the greater wisdom. As the Italian transpersonal psychologist Roberto Assagioli described it, everyone is part of a 'spiritual super-individual Reality'.[4]

Garbo approached life as a complex web of significant connections. During her early days working with Mauritz Stiller, the director would often berate her on set. Every morning he would take her for a walk, explaining his plans for the shoot. He took no interest in her opinion. In spite of this Garbo recognised their interdependence and its value. She saw her love of acting, her desire to hone her craft, as perfectly complemented by Stiller's genius and passion as a director. Garbo did not just see people, she also saw the significance of the interplay between them. She was adept at reading between the lines.

During the autumn of 1951, Garbo holidayed in England with Cecil Beaton. They divided their time between his two lavish homes. One was an elegant Georgian townhouse in Pelham Place, South Kensington. The other was Reddish House, an 18th-century manor in the village of Broad Chalke, Wiltshire. Beaton's elderly mother, Etty, was reliant on her son and spent most of her time at Reddish House. She evidently feared losing Beaton's attentions to another woman. Garbo recognised the dynamics of dependency at play in the Beaton household. During his mother's seventy-ninth birthday party, Garbo was purposefully self-effacing, blending into the background so as not to overshadow mother and son. Beaton felt this reflected Garbo's extraordinarily intuitive nature. He saw her as both tender-hearted and equitable.

George Schlee was a Russian businessman and the husband of the noted dress designer Valentina. His wife designed dresses for Garbo and other prominent actresses including Gloria Swanson and Katherine Hepburn. George became an intimate of Garbo's (much to Valentina's annoyance). He noted Garbo's non-combative nature. If a dispute with a writer or producer became heated, Garbo simply withdrew herself from the situation. For Garbo there was absolutely no value in going to war. During casting for *Queen Christina*, Garbo told Louis B. Mayer she wanted John Gilbert to play opposite her. As head of the studio Mayer was one of the most powerful men in Hollywood and unaccustomed to taking direction from his actors. On top of this, he loathed John Gilbert. Mayer was furious at Garbo's audacity. He vented his anger, bellowing at her from behind his desk. Garbo said nothing. She waited until he had run out of steam then she told him if he wasn't happy he could simply cancel the picture. She would go back to Sweden. Faced with Garbo's simple act of withdrawal, Mayer had no choice but to relent and Gilbert was given the part.

In early 1933, Garbo's friend, the actor Sven Hugo Borg, began writing features about her in the entertainment magazine *Film Pictorial*. The pair had become close friends after he had served as her interpreter when she first arrived in the US. Garbo felt that, in writing about her, he had taken advantage of their friendship and betrayed her confidence.

She and Borg arranged to meet at a restaurant in Santa Monica Canyon. Over dinner a sheepish Borg uttered numerous apologies. In an attempt to change the subject he asked Garbo how she liked being the most mysterious woman in Hollywood? She told him in ironic tones that she was not currently 'open to interviews'. In spite of this, after dinner, Garbo went back to Borg's home and stayed with him for a week. Garbo understood the interdependency between them. She knew that conflict would be pointless in this situation as surely as in any other. She made a conscious decision not to argue with him or berate him. Later, when he wrote about their meeting at the restaurant, he was entirely complimentary.

In 1979, Garbo travelled from Zurich to Paris. She was accompanied by her friend, the art dealer Sam Green. Green and Garbo met in the early seventies and he became her regular companion for the next fifteen years. On the journey to Paris they flew with the millionaire investor Élie de Rothschild in his private jet. According to biographer Barry Paris, de Rothschild's behaviour on that day was bawdy and overbearing. He made suggestive comments to Garbo throughout the journey but she did not react. Instead she lightened the tone by referring to de Rothschild good-humouredly as 'The Baron'. During the trip, Green admired Garbo's cool-handedness and the mastery with which she managed the situation. Garbo also understood the dynamics of group mentality: the way in which any mob could become so easily caught up in drama. When the Second World War broke out she chose not to take part in inflammatory discussions about the conflict.

Shooting invariably involves long periods of waiting between takes. During these times Garbo often wrote to her friend, the Swedish countess Ingrid 'Hörke' Wachtmeister. In January 1934, she wrote to Hörke describing absurd and implausible stories circulating in the press. According to the papers Garbo had got married, disappeared, shot herself, or even gone to the moon. She told Hörke she saw no point in attempting to defend herself or put the record straight. Years later, Allen Porter at the Museum of Modern Art in New York asked Garbo if he could write a series of monographs about her. She declined. He pursued the subject, suggesting it would be an opportunity to set the public straight on their many misconceptions about her. Garbo told him that sometimes the public didn't want to be set straight. As far as she was concerned, they could continue to think whatever they liked.

Garbo's self-possession served her well when faced with the many challenges of a film career. In 1925, Mauritz Stiller travelled to Istanbul with Garbo and leading man, Einar Hanson, to begin work on his next film *The Odalisque From Smolna*. A silent romantic adventure, the film was adapted from Vladimir Semitjov's novel and tells the story of a Russian woman who journeys to Constantinople in search of her long-lost lover. Stiller took full advantage of the funding from his German backers, Trianon Films. He reserved rooms at the Péra Palace, Istanbul's most luxurious hotel. He threw lavish parties. He hired a sports car and trawled the bazaars for expensive artefacts. Perhaps not surprisingly, the project folded soon after shooting had begun because Trianon Films filed for bankruptcy. Stiller dashed back to Berlin to ascertain if and when further production funds might become available. Garbo and Hanson were left stranded in Turkey. For the young Garbo, who had rarely travelled outside Sweden, this abandonment must have been frightening. The two actors were only able to travel back to Europe with the aid of the Swedish embassy. Einar Hanson was furious at being deserted by Stiller but Garbo reacted with quiet equanimity. She held firm to the belief that Stiller would rescue the situation somehow. And she was right. Ever the Houdini, Stiller had identified several alternative sources of funding including the deal with Metro-Goldwyn-Mayer that would ultimately catapult Garbo to fame.

In *Ninotchka* Garbo plays the eponymous heroine, a Soviet envoy sent to Paris to oversee the sale of jewels confiscated from Russian aristocrats. Although the serious-minded Ninotchka takes a dim view of the West, she is seduced by Count Leon d'Algout (Melvyn Douglas) and falls in love with him. Count Leon is working for the Grand Duchess Swana, one of the aristocrats trying to retrieve her confiscated jewellery. The character of Swana was played by Ina Claire, the ex-wife of John Gilbert. Garbo's past on-off romance with Gilbert was by now infamous. The potential for rivalry between the old flame and the ex-wife must have been obvious to both women, and to the studio. The pragmatic Garbo decided that animosity could be allowed no place in her working life. Making the best possible film was her primary concern. From the moment shooting began, Garbo set out to develop a firm friendship with Claire. Instead of rivals, they rapidly became collaborators. Claire was an accomplished tap dancer and Garbo even picked up a few free lessons from her.

At a party thrown by the screenwriter Salka Viertel and her director husband Berthold Viertel in the spring of 1942, Garbo met the composer David Diamond. Over the years they would spend many hours in conversation, covering almost every topic imaginable. Diamond was a classical composer considered by many to be the greatest of his generation. Diamond said that, during all their time together, he could not recall one instance of Garbo making a derogatory comment about anyone. According to Diamond she never appeared to resent anyone or anything. He saw no enmity in her, only sympathy and tenderness.

The actor Lew Ayres starred opposite Garbo in the courtroom drama, *The Kiss* (Metro-Goldwyn-Mayer, 1929), Garbo's last silent film. Garbo had loved the handsome actor's face when he screen-tested for the role of Pierre Lassalle, a young man infatuated with Garbo's character Irene. Because of Garbo's enthusiasm, Ayres was given the part immediately. In the film, the 18-year-old Pierre attempts to steal a kiss from Irene. Her husband Charles (Anders Randolf) comes home unexpectedly and catches the couple in an embrace. During the ensuing struggle, Charles is shot and killed. Irene takes the blame and stands trial for her husband's murder. When Lew Ayres was cast, it was his first acting role. He was impressed by Garbo's unshakeable composure and no-nonsense approach to the challenges of shooting. His own feelings were very different. He was nervous and intimidated by the thought of playing opposite the 'Great Garbo' (who had already made fourteen films). Garbo could easily have outperformed and outshone the greenhorn actor. She chose instead to share her expertise with him, coaching him gently on how to play to the camera. Ayres went on to become a successful film and television actor with a career that spanned seven decades. His most famous role was as the German soldier Paul Bäumer in the war film *All Quiet on the Western Front* (Universal, 1930).

Empathy between actors is not unusual. But Garbo's sense of her connectedness with others extended well beyond her immediate circle of friends and colleagues. James Rogers was a taciturn African-American originally employed by Garbo to clean her house. Rogers was a slothful character. He never hurried to perform any task. Although he was lazy, Garbo liked being in his calm, quiet presence so she asked him to be her driver as well. Unhelpfully for a driver, he struggled with telling the difference between left and right and he drove at a snail's pace. Despite his astonishing lack of gusto, Garbo felt a great affection for him and he remained in her employment for nearly a decade. To Garbo everyone in the universe was intimately connected. Garbo knew intuitively that in hurting someone else, she would only be hurting herself.

I know some very nice people in the gutter.

GARBO IN INSPIRATION
METRO-GOLDWYN-MAYER 1931

Self-actualised people see no need to label others or make generalisations about them.

In the 1920s and 30s men and women were pigeonholed into stereotypical gender roles. Man was the breadwinner, woman the homemaker. A woman was expected to set her sights on marrying the man of her dreams. Garbo defied the strict conventions of the time. She had no regard for labels or stereotypes. She certainly had no intention of following a pre-conceived notion of how she should behave or who she should love. Her romantic relationships were diverse. The Swedish Olympic swimmer Max Gumpel, the movie actress Mona Mårtensen, the French singer Marianne Oswald, the actor Sven Hugo Borg and the Metro-Goldwyn-Mayer executive Hubert Voight all enjoyed amorous entanglements with Garbo. These were aside from the two major love affairs of her life with John Gilbert and with the Spanish-American poet Mercedes de Acosta. Garbo's passion for diversity in love was also reflected in her roles on screen. In the part of Queen Christina, Garbo enjoys an intimacy with her lady-in-waiting as well as with the Spanish envoy played by John Gilbert. This sexual ambiguity was discussed by Metro-Goldwyn-Mayer producer Irving Thalberg and the film's scriptwriter Salka Viertel, Garbo's close friend. Viertel was delighted when Thalberg recommended it remain in the final draft.

Garbo portrayed many characters who defied the conventions of the times. In *The Single Standard*, Garbo plays San Francisco socialite Arden Stuart. The film opened on 27 July 1929, directed by John S. Robertson, best known for his 1920 adaptation of *Dr. Jekyll and Mr. Hyde* starring John

Barrymore. Garbo's character Arden Stuart is an early feminist archetype. In the film, she refuses to conform to disempowering gender roles. She rejects the idea that a man should have more sexual freedom than a woman: 'What difference whether girl or man? Both have the right to life.' *Susan Lenox: Her Fall And Rise* (Metro-Goldwyn-Mayer), directed by Robert Z. Leonard, premiered two years later on 16 October 1931. Garbo played the title role opposite Clark Gable (the one and only time the pair worked together). Like Arden, Susan Lenox refuses to acknowledge or respond to divisive stereotypes. When she runs away to join the circus, she is confronted by all manner of social outsiders. Society at the time would have dismissed them as 'circus freaks'. Susan embraces them all without prejudice or the need to label them. She is at ease in their company. She sees in each of them an inherent value and completeness. She expresses feelings of kinship that are fundamentally open and honest.

In a world of inequality and division, Garbo's characters were committed to fairness and justice. They identified with others beyond race and culture. They actively distanced themselves from ethnocentric thinking. Their responses to the world and the people in it suggested an appreciation of the essential unity of all humanity. In *Queen Christina*, under the direction of the Armenian-American Rouben Mamoulian, Garbo plays a woman who displays a determination to embrace different cultures and their ideas. She is told that admitting foreign professors to a Swedish university would corrupt its academic teachings. She rejects this idea firmly, suggesting instead that the university is stale precisely because of its lack of diversity. An influx of foreign scholars would refresh rather than corrupt it. She tells her traditionalist advisors, 'We need new wine in the old bottles.' In the same film she asks her lover, Don Antonio (John Gilbert), to teach her about Spanish culture. She says that to learn about it would elevate her.

The idea of universal brotherhood is also examined in *Ninotchka*, albeit from a different perspective. Blackmailed into returning to Communist Russia by Grand Duchess Swana, Ninotchka is sharing a small flat and surviving on rations. She explains to her roommate Anna (Tamara Shayne) how she is able to live beyond her means. Her friends are coming to dinner and each of them is bringing one ingredient for the meal. She says that to stand alone is to have only enough for one boiled egg. To embrace the communal spirit means having enough for a whole omelette. Off screen, Garbo held similar views. She valued plurality. She opposed segregation. These are all values associated with self-actualisation. Abraham Maslow described healthy self-actualising people as displaying an increased acceptance of others and an increased identification with the human species. There is no 'them versus us' for the self-actualised. There is instead an all-encompassing idea of 'we, together'.

Garbo was fiercely opposed to Adolf Hitler and the National Socialist German Workers' Party. In June 1933, the Jewish heavyweight boxer Max Baer defeated Hitler's favourite fighter Max Schmeling in front of a sixty thousand strong crowd at the Yankee Stadium. The Jewish Baer had brought down the Fascists' champion. He had literally given Fascism a bloody nose. The victory earned Baer the nickname of 'The Jews' Boxer'. Garbo had little interest in boxing but was overjoyed when she heard of Baer's win. She invited him to visit her on set during the making of *Queen Christina*. An invitation from Garbo was highly unusual. Even Louis B. Mayer wasn't allowed on a Garbo set. She and Baer shared an intimate lunch in her dressing room and Garbo was instantly drawn to the 6 ft 2 inch prizefighter. She saw in Baer the same values and beliefs she herself treasured. Their connection was so strong they became lovers for a time until he returned to New York for training and she began work on her next film.

When war broke out in 1939, Garbo felt compelled to act out of character, issuing a rare public statement. The statement was read to the press on her behalf by Salka Viertel. Garbo described her feelings of solidarity with all oppressed people and called herself sincerely anti-Nazi. However she would soon discover she had an unexpected and unfortunate connection to Adolf Hitler. Garbo had starred in *Camille* (Metro-Goldwyn-Mayer, 1937), a romance based on the 1848 novel by Alexandre Dumas about a French courtesan who dies tragically. It was directed by George Cukor and Garbo played opposite Robert Taylor in what is considered to be one of her greatest roles. *Camille*, Garbo discovered, was Hitler's favourite film. He even owned a personal copy. He allowed the film to be distributed across Germany in spite of the fact that its director was Jewish. He had gone as far as writing to Garbo inviting her to visit Germany. Garbo was appalled by Hitler's adulation. Her opposition to Hitler and National Socialism was so strong she once suggested to her friend Sam Green that she might be able to assassinate the Nazi leader. She claimed that she was the one person likely to be successful because her purse would not be searched. Volunteering to become an assassin seems extreme for someone so usually even tempered yet Garbo had always harboured a desire to stand up for the persecuted. During her childhood in Södermalm, the young Greta had fantasised that she might one day slay an oppressive king and replace him with a 'romantic knight'.

Garbo's contribution to the war effort was considerable but covert, made without fanfare. While Marlene Dietrich was widely known for her efforts, touring war-weary Europe to entertain the Allied troops, Garbo worked quietly behind the scenes. According to Sir William Stephenson, the head of British Security Co-ordination during World War Two, she helped identify key Nazi collaborators in Stockholm. She also contributed to Salka Viertel's efforts to rescue refugees from Nazi-occupied Europe. Garbo telephoned Niels Bohr in Stockholm, then neutral territory. Bohr was an important figure in the field of nuclear and quantum physics, and founder of the Institute of Theoretical Physics at the University of Copenhagen. Bohr had been smuggling Jewish physicists out of Germany to safe houses in Copenhagen and onto freedom in Britain or the US. In support of his efforts, Garbo called King Gustaf V of Sweden directly to ask that Bohr be given a royal audience. Bohr needed time with the Swedish King to convince him to offer asylum to Danish Jews. The King agreed and the Danish resistance movement was able to help 8,000 people escape. In all, 95% of Denmark's Jewish population survived the Holocaust. At Garbo's request, Sir William Stephenson ensured personally that Bohr found safety in Britain. After the war Bohr went on to play a key role in establishing CERN, the European organisation for nuclear research.

Garbo's feelings of solidarity with the disadvantaged and persecuted were rooted in her childhood experiences. Heralding from an impoverished family in the slums of Stockholm, Garbo had bitter experience of being at the lower end of the social hierarchy. A family of five, the Gustafssons were squeezed into a tiny three room flat with no hot water. The children often went hungry. But Greta never gave in to resentment or bitterness. It led her instead to believe in a universal principle of equality and fairness. Her egalitarianism embraced everyone from the poorest to the most socially privileged. She did not reverence rank or title, no matter how elevated. When Garbo was holidaying with Cecil Beaton in the summer of 1951, he introduced her to Princess Margaret. The two women hit it off instantly. Garbo thought no differently of an English princess than she did of the local shopkeeper in Beaton's village. In fact, she struck up a warm friendship with him too and with the local parish priest. She enjoyed hearing the striking regional accents and encountering the singularity of Wiltshire country ways in Broad Chalke village.

After the end of the Second World War, the French Riviera became popular as the gayest and most beautiful resort in the world. Palm trees and semi-tropical plants lined the boulevards and red rocks jutted out into cobalt blue seas. While holidaying there in 1950, Garbo became friends with the Swedish count Carl Johan Bernadotte and his wife Kerstin. Because Kerstin was not of royal blood, Carl Johan had surrendered his succession rights to the Swedish throne to marry her. The parallels between Carl Johan's story and the narrative of *Queen Christina* were uncanny and would not have been lost on Garbo. Throughout her life, Garbo held firm to the belief that one should be free to love whoever one pleased. She spent time with Carl Johan and Kerstin Bernadotte again in 1975, staying at their villa in the Swedish coastal town of Bastad. Garbo befriended the neighbourhood farmer Ivar Nilsson. Both shared a love of the natural world. No matter how many movies she made, no matter how famous she became, she never lost sight of the principle that all people were equal members of the family of humanity.

In the autumn of 1975, Garbo was invited to tea at Buckingham Palace. She was spending a month in London on holiday with Sam Green. The invitation was handed to Green as he and Garbo returned to their Piccadilly apartment after a brief shopping expedition to Fortnum and

Mason. Up in their rented rooms, Green poured Garbo a drink and revealed that the game was up - although they had been careful to avoid the press and had dined in the flat every night, her presence in London had been discovered. He gave her the invitation. It was signed E.R. and assured Garbo, 'You will be alone.' Garbo handed it back to Green. She told him she couldn't possibly go because she didn't have a thing to wear. She said he was more than welcome to go on his own if he liked. Though flattering, the royal invitation was not part of the plans Garbo had already made for herself - to spend some quiet, contemplative time hidden away in the big city. She was not interested in meeting the British Head of State for the sake of it. Her meeting with Princess Margaret had been an impromptu one. She had enjoyed the princess's company not because she was royalty but because, like Garbo, she was a free spirit. A formal invitation to Buckingham Palace lacked the spontaneity and warmth of her earlier royal encounter. Garbo had no difficulty, at all, in turning down an invitation from the Queen of England.

I shall always dress for dinner.

GARBO IN THE TEMPTRESS
METRO-GOLDWYN-MAYER 1926

Self-actualised people are comfortable with who they are.

Existentialism identifies creatureliness and godlikeness as the two principal opposing forces of human nature. Creatureliness involves accepting one's own humanity with all its imperfections. Godlikeness involves striving towards a higher spiritual consciousness. The surest path to inner peace involves a synthesis of the two. Only through this synthesis can there be a more solid sense of self, a knowledge and acceptance of one's own inherent nature. Self-actualised people are increasingly able to attain this synthesis. It allows them an intrinsic congruence where their outer and inner selves match. They have no need to impress, no need to pretend they are something they are not. Who they are on the inside and who they present to the outside world are one and the same. The self-actualised are able to function effortlessly with a sense of self that is complete. Consequently they are not defined by other people. They do not feel deficient in any way or in need of 'shoring up' from the outside. They inhabit their own skin with consummate ease.

Louis B. Mayer met Garbo for the first time in November 1924. He was in Europe dealing with production problems on the biblical epic *Ben Hur*. He was travelling with his wife and daughter and invited Garbo and Mauritz Stiller to join his family for dinner. He was keen to meet Garbo because he had seen her in a screening of Stiller's romantic drama *Gösta Berlings Saga*, an adaptation of the debut novel of Swedish author and Nobel prizewinner Selma Lagerlöf. When Mayer first watched the film, he had been struck not by Garbo's beauty but by the expression in her eyes. The Mayers met Garbo and Stiller for dinner at the Adlon in Berlin, one of Europe's most impressive and luxurious hotels. On first meeting Garbo, Louis B. Mayer's daughter Irene was unimpressed. Irene recalls how unremarkable Garbo was. She did not stand out in any way. Irene felt that Garbo failed to put on a convincing show for her father. Irene had misinterpreted one of the most fundamental aspects of Garbo's character: she did not feel the need to put on a show for anyone or to dance to anyone else's tune. She was fully realised and secure in her self. This quality of self-containment was what had inspired Irene's father to pursue Garbo in the first place. This was what he had first noticed on her face in the screening room. It was this he had detected in Garbo's eyes.

During her early days in Hollywood, it was Mayer alone who grasped the uniqueness of Garbo. The publicist Howard Dietz was as unimpressed as Irene Mayer. The movie mogul Nicholas Schenk couldn't even find the time to meet her and Metro-Goldwyn-Mayer Vice President Edward Bowes predicted she would be heading back to Sweden in less than six months. Perhaps her co-star in *Torrent*, Ricardo Cortez, also saw something of what Louis B. Mayer saw. But his jealousy of Garbo prevented him from acknowledging it at the time. It wasn't until 1965, in an interview with film historian Kevin Brownlow, that Cortez admitted to having seen the hidden depth in Garbo's eyes: 'The structure of the eyes, I think, is what people were attracted to. Strange quality - introverted, electric.'[5] Garbo's power derived from her honest relationship with her own flawed humanity and her striving for something higher, something transcendent. In his biography of Garbo, Barry Paris describes her distinct blend of passion and detachment. It was as if she were two people at once - a participant and an observer inhabiting the same body. It was as if she contained, at one and the same time, both a still, universal awareness and a moving, embodied awareness. The psychologist Roberto Assagioli described this state of calm involved detachment as the ability to 'make haste slowly'. To achieve this state is to become 'almost dual, the one who acts, and the one who simultaneously looks on as the observer.'[6] It was precisely this synthesis of the observer and the observed, the detached and the involved, that gave Garbo the power to inhabit fully and frankly the characters she portrayed. It also provided a firm foundation of self-awareness and security for the young woman destined to become Garbo.

In the Stockholm of 1921, as a youngster with a burning desire to act, it was Greta who first sought out Mauritz Stiller. As he parked his bright yellow Kissel motor car outside his home, she strode up and asked him for an audition. He told her to come back when she was a little older. She had more success later the same year when she approached the film-maker Ragnar Ring. Having found out where he lived, she went to see him during her lunch break. Ring was making a clothes commercial called *How Not to*

Dress for Greta's then employer PUB department store. He was sufficiently impressed by her boldness to offer her the comic role of an awkward girl in ill-fitting clothes who gorges herself on cakes and biscuits. Garbo employed similar tactics whenever she saw the potential for a new friendship. She met Salka Viertel for the first time in 1930 at a party thrown by Ernst Lubitsch. Salka and her husband Berthold were members of the Jewish-German intelligentsia. Salka was self-assured and physically strong. Garbo was immediately taken with this confident woman and wanted to know her better. The day after the party, the doorbell rang at Salka's house in Santa Monica. She answered the door to find Garbo standing there. Garbo coolly announced her wish to continue their conversation from the night before. The two women spent the entire afternoon together, walking slowly along the beach and sharing their passions for life and art as they returned to Salka's home. Any of these unconventional encounters could have ended in rebuttal and a bruised ego for Garbo but that possibility did not deter her. Her willingness to take straightforward, decisive action sprang from the security afforded by her clearly developed sense of self.

Both the media and the public expected Garbo to get married eventually. Speculation was most intense around her on-off romance with John Gilbert. Even when hounded by reporters eager for a scoop, Garbo refused to fuel the rumours of her imminent engagement. Ever since her student days at the Royal Dramatic Academy in Stockholm, she had been adamant that marriage was not for her. She told actor Nils Asther that she had no intention of marrying ever. She had decided to dedicate herself, not to a man, but to her art: to film and to the theatre. This sentiment is echoed in *Queen Christina* when Garbo's Christina tells her Lord Chancellor she will not marry: 'I have no intention to Chancellor. I shall die a bachelor.' Christina's dedication to her country echoes Garbo's dedication to her craft. Christina refuses to marry in order to avoid conflicts of interest, distractions or a lessening of her focus. Similarly Garbo would remain single, self-contained, sufficient unto herself and dedicated, without distractions, to deepening her understanding of her craft.

The less notice she took of the world, the more obsessed the world became with her. Heedless of the waiting paparazzi, she rarely wore make-up outside the studio. Her Lincoln motor car was simple and conventional. Her choice was markedly different from Hollywood actresses like Joan Crawford who preferred luxury models such as the Cadillac Fleetwood and the V-16 Town Car. Her home was similarly unostentatious. It might even be described as austere. When her lover Mercedes de Acosta came to stay, they dined on bread, cheese and milk in Garbo's bedroom. Mercedes was particularly struck by this aspect of Garbo's personality. She saw Garbo as an artist devoted only to making works of art. In her memoirs, Mercedes likens the identity of a great artist to that of a mystic: 'All true artists, like all true mystics (who are in a sense artists transformed to a higher level), have illumination to a lesser or a greater degree.'[7] Garbo was happy with the simple life she led. Her dress sense was original and unconventional. She wore a signature straw gardening hat and slacks most days. In bed, she wore what she liked to describe as a pair of old man's pyjamas. No one could accuse Garbo of taking herself too seriously. The press could not mould her into the celebrity they wanted her to be. She was too independent minded, too sure of herself. For these crimes, journalists punished her. They portrayed her as tragic, husbandless and lonely. They had no interest in looking beneath the surface to reveal the woman of strong character and determination. When she first arrived in Hollywood her English was limited and her command of German was of little use. Rather than seeing this as a liability, Garbo turned her broken English into a charming attribute. On more than one occasion, Salka Viertel remarked how endearing it was whenever Garbo made fun of herself for the way she spoke. Yet this light-hearted side of Garbo was not well known by those beyond her inner circle. When Pamela Mason, wife of actor James Mason, first met Garbo in 1949, she was unprepared for her quirky sense of humour. The two women met when Garbo visited James Mason's home to discuss collaborating on *La Duchesse de Langeais*, an ultimately doomed film project based on the novel by Honoré de Balzac. Garbo struck Pamela Mason as the antithesis of the introverted and lonely figure depicted by the newspapers. She described Garbo as light-hearted, full of fun and, in typical Garbo style, not wearing a dash of make-up. Garbo was always likely to do what was least expected of her. Her second Hollywood film was a silent romantic drama called *The Temptress* (Metro-Goldwyn-Mayer, 1926), directed by Fred Niblo. Garbo plays the vampish Elena who follows her lover Robledo (Antonio Moreno) to South America. Robledo tells her Argentina is a country of work and hardship where people simply do not dress for dinner. Garbo replies, 'I shall always dress for dinner.'

When she visited Cecil Beaton's New York hotel room in the spring of 1946, Beaton observed how she was instantly able to make the room her own. There was an apparent surety in the way she moved through the world. Her personality had developed into an unusual blend of vibrancy and serenity. She 'made haste slowly' in the words of Roberto Assagioli. Even in the high drama of her films she is nevertheless a centre of stillness. In 1930, the film critic Mordaunt Hall, writing in *The New York Times*, noted Garbo's intensity of expression and measured movement on screen. The author Robert E. Sherwood, writing in *Life* magazine, paid tribute to her power to fascinate, declaring her the 'Official Dream Princess'. Jane Perry Gunther, the editor of *Reader's Digest*, summed up Garbo's otherworldly presence most succinctly: 'She has a poetic magic, so difficult to describe, and all one knows is that one wants this in one's life.'[8]

I have nothing to reproach myself with. And I am indifferent to public opinion.

GARBO IN THE KISS
METRO-GOLDWYN-MAYER 1929

Self-actualised people recognise their own worth.

Garbo told her friend and biographer Raymond Daum that she really wanted two lives - one for the movies and one for herself. She found her fans' intensity psychologically unnerving. She did not understand what they hoped to gain by writing to her. They were not her family, she reasoned. They did not know her personally. They had no idea who she really was. Why did they want her picture? She was a down-to-earth Swede. Swedes did not naturally indulge in this kind of fanaticism and it was simply alien to her. Almost certainly, Garbo would have been similarly perplexed by Facebook or Twitter and it's safe to say she would not have signed up to either. The Metro-Goldwyn-Mayer PR department once suggested it would be good publicity for Garbo to become the face of Palmolive soap. Garbo responded by saying that the best publicity of all was a well made film. She knew her worth as an actress. Her real reason for going to America was to play interesting roles and to make films of the highest quality. Otherwise, she wanted as little fuss as possible and certainly had no interest in joining her Hollywood peers, treated like gods on a tinsel Mount Olympus. When shooting finished on a film, she often decamped to Sweden for months at a time. She regularly stayed at Tistad Castle, the home of her friends Countess Hörke and Count Nils Wachtmeister. These extended breaks enabled her to find a secluded corner of the world where she would not be disturbed. Garbo was always happy for someone else to be the centre of attention. She avoided the many extravagant soirées hosted by celebrities such as party-girl actress Marion Davies and bloated gossip columnist Elsa Maxwell. Garbo would never refuse an invitation but when the night of the party came, she simply would not go. When a party was in full swing, nobody was concerned with the absentees. She even avoided parties thrown in her honour. On 26 July 1926, when shooting wrapped for *The Temptress*, a film in which she plays a pleasure-seeking vamp, she did not attend the post-production party. Instead she threw a private birthday party for her friends Sven Hugo Borg and Lars Hanson.

Garbo did not seek the approval of others but this freeing approach to life also came at a price. The more she shied away from the spotlight the more the spotlight was focused on her. It is a simple fact of human nature that people always want what they can't have. The more they couldn't have Garbo, the more they wanted her. The mystery surrounding her was fuelled by her own desire to keep her private life out of the public domain. In 1937, she purchased a farm at Lake Gillen, forty miles south of Stockholm. As soon as the legal papers were signed, she moved her mother, her older brother Sven, his wife and children into the property. Her intention was twofold. She wanted to own a retreat in rural Sweden and she wanted to provide her family with a home far removed from the Stockholm slums of her youth. She was dismayed when she learned that a photographer named Emilie Danielson had taken photos of the property. Unfortunately for Garbo, Danielson sold the pictures to *Movie Mirror* and the magazine soon lifted the lid on the secret hideaway of the woman it called the 'Viking Venus'.

This particular 'Viking Venus' felt no need to protest her status or intelligence. Only her closest friends knew just how cultivated she actually was. Through her relationship with John Gilbert, she got to know Carey Wilson, the screenwriter of *Ben Hur*. At the time, Wilson was separated from his wife and living at Gilbert's house. Wilson and Garbo spent many hours discussing topics as diverse as the science of radio transmission and the plays of Henrik Ibsen. Wilson confessed he was surprised at the extent of Garbo's literary knowledge. Garbo became a frequent guest at Salka Viertel's home. The Viertel's Sunday afternoon salon was a meeting place for German intellectual émigrés including Thomas Mann, Berthold Brecht and Arnold Schoenberg. Garbo once told Max Reinhardt how much she wanted to play Hamlet. Salka and Garbo were both, in essence, foreigners in the United States and as outsiders, they naturally gravitated towards each other. They discussed music, sculpture and the theatre. They rarely discussed Hollywood.

The film premiere was a convention of the film industry that Garbo particularly disliked. The thought of walking the red carpet in front of screaming crowds made her intensely uncomfortable. It was just one more example of the cultish treatment of actors that she found disproportionate and embarrassing. When she and Mauritz Stiller attended the Berlin premiere for *Gösta Berlings Saga*, Garbo made sure she knew one phrase in German, 'Ich gehe jetzt,' meaning, 'I'm going now.' When her first Hollywood movie, *Torrent*, premiered in February 1926 in New York and then in Los Angeles, Garbo was conspicuous by her absence. This set the trend for the rest of her career. She only ever attended one Hollywood premiere and it was for somebody else's film. *Bardelys the Magnificent* (Metro-Goldwyn-Mayer, 1926), a silent adaptation of the 1906 romantic novel by Rafael Sabatini, starred Garbo's lover John Gilbert in the title role. Garbo accompanied Gilbert to the premiere in September 1926, just seven months after *Torrent*. Disquieted by the circus on the red carpet, she made a swift departure as soon as the film was over and declined to go to the after-party at the famous Cocoanut Grove night club. When Garbo did attend a screening of one of her films, it was usually as a regular moviegoer. Disguised in a hat and trench coat she would buy a ticket to watch the film at her local cinema. She took a mischievous delight in the audience being unaware that she was sitting among them.

Later in life, even though she hadn't made a film for over thirty years, Garbo still took steps to protect her anonymity. During the 1970s, when she was living on New York's East Fifty-second Street, she meticulously avoided photographers. It was not because she felt past her prime and did not want to be photographed. She simply believed that every time she was pictured in the press, she became easier to spot when she was out walking in the city. If people recognised her and asked her for an autograph, she always refused. This was not to be unkind. She saw it purely as an unwarranted intrusion on her privacy. She did not have an ego that craved attention. As an egalitarian Swede, she felt that people were effacing themselves when they placed her on a pedestal.

She was equally fair-minded in her relationships with her co-stars. Although she had top billing, she did not regard herself as more important than the rest of the cast. During the filming of the 1941 comedy, *Two-Faced Woman*, the English actor Roland Young asked her to sign a photograph. She politely turned him down. She had been so supportive on set that Young kept the unsigned photo anyway. When she donated to the Finnish Relief Fund in 1939, she did so anonymously. She wanted no special attention. Other people were supporting the same fund. Her contribution was no more significant than theirs.

One of the first directors to work with Garbo, Ragnar Ring, criticised her for not offering a smile and some friendly words to reporters. Garbo thought it wiser not to encourage what she regarded as hysteria and foolish 'fuss'. She saw no reason why she should answer personal questions from people she did not know. Garbo has often been misquoted as saying she wanted to be alone. What she actually said was, 'I want to be let alone,' a comment aimed squarely at the press. Because it didn't suit their purposes, journalists simply changed her words. Every time Garbo travelled back to Europe she was hounded by reporters. She travelled under pseudonyms such as Alice Smith, Miss Swanson or Mrs Gustafsson. When sailing from New York to Sweden, she would remain in her stateroom for the duration of the voyage. Reporters chased Garbo and Hörke Wachtmeister across London and Paris in the winter of 1932, eager for a few words and a photograph. In both cities Garbo eluded them. Finally, in June 1936, she wearily agreed to a ten-minute press conference aboard the Swedish ocean liner, Gripsholm. Reporters expecting to be ushered into a spacious auditorium were disappointed. Garbo requested that the session take place in the ship's smoking room. She answered their questions for ten minutes. No more.

Garbo was unimpressed by status. In this regard she was consistent to the end. In the course of her career, she turned down several European royals when they asked to visit her on set. In 1937, when she was awarded the Swedish royal medal for outstanding contributions to dramatic art, Garbo did not attend the ceremony. The medal was to be presented by the Swedish Consul at a grand event in San Francisco before a large audience. She asked that the medal be sent to her in the post. Garbo was equally unstirred by great names in the world of art. When the celebrated constructivist artist Joseph Cornell made a Garbo portrait box for his 1942 exhibition at the Museum of Modern Art in New York, Garbo was unimpressed. She felt the portrait bore only the vaguest resemblance to her. Cornell subsequently dismantled it.

Garbo appeared in *Inspiration* as Yvonne Valbret, an artists' model and a kept woman. The film was directed by Clarence Brown and based on the 1884 novella, *Sappho*, by

Alphonse Daudet. In the role of her lover, Robert Montgomery tells Garbo she is so beautiful he wishes he could always see her across the breakfast table. Garbo replies, 'Always is a dangerous word.' In the steamy romantic drama, *Flesh And The Devil* (Metro-Goldwyn-Mayer, 1926) also directed by Brown, John Gilbert tells her they should see each other often. Garbo answers him, 'Perhaps.'

Garbo was always a little cautious or reserved with friends and lovers. When he first met Garbo, Sam Green confessed that he had never seen one of her films and knew little about her. Perhaps this was the reason that she told him straightaway she knew they would be friends. Sometimes her cool independence exasperated the people closest to her. In his memoirs, Cecil Beaton describes sending her a stream of telegrams and telephoning her house numerous times. He admits to becoming increasingly frustrated as she remained steadfastly silent. One might suggest that Garbo knew full well how desirable her elusiveness made her. Beaton's friend Mona Harrison Williams suggested he give Garbo a taste of her own medicine. Beaton ceased phoning and sending telegrams. Within a few days, it was Garbo who contacted *him*. The experience gave Beaton a glimpse of the inner workings of Garbo's power. Her role as the self-styled queen of unavailability simply served to make friends, lovers, fans and the media long for her ever more intensely.

*I've heard
so much
about you.
I know
we will
be friends.*

GARBO TO SAM GREEN
18 SEPTEMBER 1970

Self-actualised people recognise the value in other human beings.

Contrary to popular belief, Garbo had no desire to hide away from other people. She enjoyed the company of friends just as much as anybody else. George Cukor, who directed two of Garbo's films, described her as a woman who liked people, but usually just one at a time. Garbo was a great listener. She liked to give her undivided attention and this was best achieved on a one-to-one basis. The theatre critic Kenneth Tynan was first introduced to Garbo by Cecil Beaton in 1954. He described their meeting in an article for the film journal *Sight and Sound*. According to Tynan, Garbo asked him a multitude of questions about his life with the infectious eagerness of a person who had just landed from Mars. Her ability to pay close attention to others made Garbo a shrewd judge of people. Salka Viertel described her ability to make canny assessments of others. Mauritz Stiller was often dismissed as no more than an outlandish figure. Wearing coloured waistcoats, ankle length fur coats and dripping in jewellery, he stood out in any crowd. Yet Garbo was not misled by his outward appearance. She was able to perceive the man behind the facade, a consummate writer and director. She was able to see his potential to help her. Vera Schmiterlow, Garbo's former lover and Royal Academy classmate, observed that Garbo willingly became the raw material that Stiller shaped into form. From losing weight to choosing a new name, Garbo eagerly took her mentor's advice.

Garbo also had a deep admiration for the German director F.W. Murnau. In March 1931, Murnau was killed in a car accident while performing oral sex on his underage Polynesian chauffeur. Murnau's death ignited an intense public scandal. When the day of his funeral came, most of his friends chose to stay away. Only eleven people had the courage to attend the ceremony. Garbo was one of them. In spite of the scandal - and the risks of being publicly associated with it - she held true to her original judgement of Murnau's value as a friend. The characters Garbo portrayed were often equally acute in their assessment of other people. In the titular role of Anna Christie, a woman with a hidden past as a prostitute, Garbo decides she cannot marry her beau. She is able to see him for what he is - an innocent. She says he is a simple guy, a big kid. Even though it would be easy to do so, she cannot bring herself to deceive him about her chequered past. In *Romance* (Metro-Goldwyn-Mayer, 1930), Garbo plays Rita Cavallini, an acclaimed New York opera singer at the pinnacle of her career. Rita has an artist's heightened perceptive abilities, so much so that she is able to intuit a person's character simply by looking at his or her likeness in a photograph.

Garbo built and maintained a small circle of close friends who she held in high regard. She once told Cecil Beaton that she had few friends but they always stuck. For Garbo, a small number of devoted friends was preferable to a large number of casual ones. Salka Viertel, George Schlee, Cécile de Rothschild and Aristotle Onassis all at various times formed part of Garbo's inner circle. She was never territorial about her friendships. She was happy for her friends to know one another. Hörke and Nils Wachtmeister were two of the people closest to her. Garbo regularly brought other friends to stay with the Wachtmeisters when she visited them at Tistad, south of Stockholm. Because Garbo invested in a small number of important friendships, she was able to devote a larger share of her attention to each of her friends and she treated them very well. Whenever she was in Sweden, she would make a point of catching up with all of her friends there. No one would be left out. Friends like the Wachtmeisters became intensely loyal to her and they were instrumental in helping her find her farmhouse hideaway at Hårby, southwest of Stockholm. She took the opinions of her friends very seriously and always followed up their recommendations to read a particular author they liked and admired. She was interested in 19th-century Russian novelists as well as Goethe and the Romantic poets. She was similarly conscientious when friends recommended plays or films. As George Schlee remarked in an article for the illustrated journal *Collier's*, 'She will read anything recommended by someone she respects.'[9]

Even when people acted in a hurtful way, Garbo rarely allowed the situation to escalate to the point that a relationship became irredeemable. Throughout her life she attempted to keep her personal life away from the prying eyes of the media. When Sven Hugo Borg broke her trust and wrote about her in his column she forgave him. She did the same when Cecil Beaton betrayed her confidence, first by publishing thirteen private photographic portraits in the July 1946 edition of *Vogue* and later by revealing details about their relationship in *The Happy Years*, a volume of memoirs he published in the summer of 1972. Garbo did not always forgive quickly but she was prepared to forgive in the end.

When people needed help she was always willing to offer a hand. There were several elderly actors in the cast of *The Painted Veil* (Metro-Goldwyn-Mayer,1934). During filming, storm sequences required the set to be doused in water. Garbo insisted the elderly actors had comfortable chairs set aside for them in a dry part of the stage. She was similarly attentive to the needs of younger actors. During the making of *The Kiss*, directed by Jacques Feyder, she coached her eager but nervous young co-star Lew Ayres to deliver his lines with more confidence. Ayres gained invaluable acting skills from Garbo's tuition and the pair remained friends for many years. When Roland Young worked with Garbo in *Two-Faced Woman*, he noted that she still helped other actors learn their lines even though she had been Hollywood's most important star for almost two decades. Garbo was drawn to talented people but she was never jealous of their talent or expected to gain from her friendship with them. She was attracted to Mercedes de Acosta because she was an accomplished feminist, poet and Theosophist. These characteristics spoke to Garbo's interest in strong and cultured women as well as her interest in the occult. She was drawn to the Canadian actor Marie Dressler because of her skill as a performer. Dressler was a formidable and experienced comedy actress with a tousled mop of dark hair and sparkling eyes. Garbo was so impressed by Dressler's performance in *Anna Christie*, she was determined to show the elderly actor the depth of her admiration. After shooting wrapped, she went to Dressler's house and presented her with a giant bunch of yellow chrysanthemums. One of the reasons Garbo so disliked Louis B. Mayer was because of the way he treated Dressler. In 1933, while working on Metro-Goldwyn-Mayer's comedy-drama *Dinner at Eight*, Dressler was taken ill and Mayer insisted his own doctor examine her. The doctor told Mayer that Dressler was suffering from an incurable form of cancer. Mayer withheld this diagnosis from her to ensure she continued working. When he eventually revealed the truth, he promised her $100,000 if she would complete the two remaining pictures in her contract, *Tugboat Annie* and *Christopher Bean*. Dressler agreed. She wanted a portion of the money to go to her maid and also to help set up an African-American community centre. But after filming was completed, Mayer broke his promise and only gave Dressler $10,000. She died shortly afterwards in July 1934. Garbo could never forgive Mayer for his manipulative and dishonest treatment of a woman she admired.

Garbo appreciated talent in others without feeling threatened by it. When she and Joan Crawford began shooting on the set of *Grand Hotel* (Metro-Goldwyn-Mayer, 1932), Crawford was a rising star. She was beautiful, driven and politically astute. As Garbo walked past on set one day,

Crawford even remarked to the columnist Sara Hamilton, 'There goes my ambition. When Garbo leaves... I'll be able to take over.' Despite Crawford's notorious ambitiousness, Garbo showed no reticence or insecurity on their first meeting. By contrast, Crawford was visibly flustered and tongue-tied. Garbo told Crawford warmly she was delighted they were working together and asked her how she was getting on. Later press reports of antagonism between the two women were totally unfounded, a fabrication to sell newspapers and movie magazines.

Between takes on *Grand Hotel*, Garbo kissed her co-star Lionel Barrymore suddenly on the lips. The Academy Award-winning actor came from a distinguished acting family that included Georgina Drew Barrymore and John Barrymore. Garbo told him passionately how honoured she felt to be playing opposite so perfect an artist. Words, when spoken with authenticity and conviction, have the power to cement transcending relationships.

Holidaying in the south of France in the summer of 1947, Garbo was introduced to Cecil Beaton's friends Michael Duff and David Herbert. When she learned that they had fought against the Nazis in the war, she told them how wonderful it was to meet two men who had helped save the world. Her comments could also be disarmingly playful. In July 1946, Garbo was besieged by fans outside Stockholm Central Station. She was guided to safety by a policeman named John Engberg. As he swept her towards Max Gumpel's waiting car, she leaned into him and told him it was a long time since she had held the arm of such a fine looking fellow.

Equally, Garbo understood the harm that words could do. For example, she never revealed secrets about her fiery relationship with John Gilbert. When asked her opinion of Gilbert, she described him simply as a man of temperament but equally one of the finest men she had ever known. She would not be drawn into revealing anything more. She was similarly discreet in all her relationships. When King Carl XVI Gustav and Queen Silvia of Sweden visited New York in 1987, they hoped for the chance to meet Garbo. Surprisingly she agreed. The meeting took place at her apartment in Manhattan and lasted three-quarters of an hour. They drank tea and chatted about everyday things like the New York weather. They did not discuss the movies and the press were not allowed in. The story would have been a journalist's dream, the King and Queen of Sweden meet the Swedish Queen of Hollywood. Afterwards Queen Sylvia described Garbo as 'magical'. Garbo, naturally, said nothing at all.

She was equally taciturn when it came to talking about her own family. She did not want them subjected to the same media intrusions she was forced to endure. In Garbo's eyes, her family life was of no more interest than anyone else's. She had a mother. She had a father. Her family lived in a house. That was all anybody needed to know. When her brother Sven tried his hand at acting and changed his name to Sven Garbo, she was not impressed. She feared his attempt to gain recognition for himself as Greta Garbo's brother would threaten the family privacy she had worked so hard to maintain. She needn't have worried. His film career comprised just three films and lasted barely two years from 1929 to 1930. Universally unloved by the critics, his only distinction was that he appeared in the first Swedish language talkie, *När Rosorna Slå Ut / When the Roses Bloom* (Paramount Pictures, 1930), a treasure hunt drama directed by Edvin Adolphson.

Garbo's was not the life of the tragic misanthrope. She had solid friendships. She appreciated genius in others. She repaid kindness with kindness. She did not participate in power play with her rivals. She engaged with friends and colleagues in an open and honest way. These were all vital aspects of the spirit of Garbo.

Lonely? I've never been so contented in my life.

GARBO IN INSPIRATION
METRO-GOLDWYN-MAYER 1931

Self-actualised people are unperturbed by silence or solitude.

The popular culture and news magazine *Liberty* was launched by McCormick-Patterson on 10 May 1924. The magazine featured regular contributions from notable figures in the worlds of politics, literature and entertainment. Among them were Gandhi, Churchill, Agatha Christie and Jean Harlow. Towards the end of the 1920s, the magazine asked Garbo for a contribution. On this occasion she agreed, perhaps because she wanted to say something of particular significance to the life of an artist. She wrote about the constant pressure to attend Hollywood parties and events and how this caused her work to suffer. In her opinion, the creative artist should be a rare and solitary spirit. Being alone held no anxiety for her nor did it foster in her the need to seek company. To Garbo solitude was Elysian. Like a fervent eremite, she actively pursued opportunities to be quiet and on her own. Garbo's essential, solitary nature imparted to her a transcendent and ethereal quality, a suggestion of otherness. The prolific Hollywood costume designer Adrian described her beauty as being essentially spiritual. Mercedes de Acosta proclaimed Garbo to be a radiant goddess of the elements.

At just eighteen years old, when shooting finished on *Gösta Berlings Saga*, Garbo left Stockholm for the western Swedish county of Värmland. There she rented an isolated cottage and spent her days roaming in the vast and unspoilt Scandinavian countryside. Solitary communion with nature was something she cherished. It grounded her and distanced her from Hollywood and its attendant artifice. It also allowed her to exist, for a time at least, in deep sympathy with the elements. When she was in Hollywood, she would ask her driver, James, to take her out to Lake Arrowhead. Surrounded by the San Bernadino mountains, she would row out into the middle of the lake and remain there for hours, completely alone. In her final film, *Two-Faced Woman*, Garbo plays ski instructor Karin Borg. At the beginning of the film, Karin declares her intention to settle down to a quiet life in the beautiful snow-capped mountains. Garbo would often head into the mountains at Casa Del Mar in Santa Monica. Sitting on a mountaintop, she would look out over the vastness of the ocean, absorbing its tranquillity.

Equally, Garbo had no reservations about living on her own. She decided at an early age that married life was not for her. In 1928, when asked by the writer Rilla Page Palmborg about her rocky relationship with John Gilbert, Garbo described her overwhelming desire to be on her own: 'It is a friendship. I will never marry.'[10] For Garbo, this was a conscious choice rather than a predicament. She was happy to be single. She did not need anybody to complete her. She was complete in herself. The only companion she needed was Mother Nature. At the height of her career, while living at 1027 Chevy Chase Drive, she would rise early and go to the nearby riding stables to walk in the countryside. She loved the wild power of nature and liked to walk in heavy rainstorms until she was soaking wet. She was not prey to the same feelings of isolation as other people because she had a profound connection to the planet earth and to the wider universe. The undisturbed vastness of the natural world provided a counterbalance to the turbulence of human affairs. She disliked arguing or witnessing arguments. In her films she refused to take part in scenes that involved fighting. On her first journey from Stockholm to New York aboard the cruise ship Drottningholm in June 1925, Garbo described the immense emptiness of the ocean and experiencing the bliss of perfect solitude. This is the peak experience of the self-actualised individual, a moment where, as Abraham Maslow put it, all sense of separateness from the world disappears. Several years later Garbo took a leisurely journey aboard the Annie Johnson, a freighter en route from Scandinavia to San Diego via the Panama Canal. The trip lasted for an entire month. Although her cabin was basic, she relished the opportunity to be solitary and to experience time moving at a slower pace.

In 1932, Garbo vanished suddenly. A simple wish for solitude lay behind her dramatic disappearance. When shooting wrapped on *As You Desire Me* (Metro-Goldwyn-Mayer, 1932), an adaptation of Luigi Pirandello's mystery play, Garbo disappeared for a total of eight months. Reporters eventually found her at a secluded lakeside villa one hour outside of Stockholm. She had passed the time taking long walks and rowing on the lake. Garbo was never bored or at a loss during her extended solitary breaks. She remarked to the journalist Julia Svenson that she was not aloof or snobbish as some Hollywood pundits had painted her. She simply liked to be by herself because quiet time allowed her to renew her energies. She took far more pleasure in reading a good book or listening to the radio than attending even the most agreeable of Hollywood gatherings. She was someone who liked to live simply, dress simply and have time for actively doing nothing.

In *Anna Karenina*, Countess Vronsky (May Robson) describes Garbo's Anna as having the divine gift of silence. To Garbo, a gap in conversation was never something that cried out to be filled. She would only speak when something worth saying occurred to her. Sometimes Garbo invited Mercedes over to her Santa Monica home and for long periods the two women would sit in silence under the eucalyptus trees in the garden. In the summer of 1931, they spent six weeks at a remote cabin in the Sierra Nevadas. They would go boating and sit quietly together on the still water. They would not exchange a word. Silence strengthened the connection between them. As Mercedes commented in her memoir *Here Lies the Heart*, 'In all this time there was not a second of disharmony between Greta and me or in nature around us.' Later she wrote, 'The days and hours flew past far too quickly. They did more than that. They evaporated. There was no sense of time at all.'[11] Garbo was drawn to people who were as relaxed with silence as she was. She enjoyed spending time with Aristotle Onassis because of his charm and intelligence, the straight-forwardness of their friendship and his silences. But not all of Garbo's friends felt so comfortable. The conductor

Leopold Stokowski holidayed with her in Italy, North Africa and Sweden between February and July 1938. He enjoyed lengthy discussions on philosophy but was self-conscious when it came to prolonged silences between them. In many ways silence was like a place of refuge for Garbo. Confronted by a problem, she did not deal with it by lamenting or complaining. For her, the answer was to be found in silence and contemplation. Mercedes described this as letting 'the mind rest quietly on the Self in the cave of the Spiritual Heart'.[12] Silence also allowed Garbo a private inner space in which to perfect her craft. In *Here Lies the Heart*, Mercedes recalls walking with Garbo after a long day of filming. Walking was one of Garbo's favourite pastimes. She would walk in all weathers along the beach or in the hills. According to Mercedes, she would often walk in silence, contemplating a character she was playing or connecting spiritually with the scenario she would later have to perform. Mercedes described these as moments where Garbo would go 'into her inner self'. She never portrayed a character. She became the character. She inhabited the character's soul. She achieved this through the inspiration she found deep in the core of her being. In an article credited to Garbo in 1929, she describes a method of calming the mind through focused thought and relaxation. It involves lying on a couch, closing the eyes, relaxing the muscles and visualising pleasant things. The session lasts for twenty minutes after which there is a feeling of being free and refreshed. Later on in life, Garbo became interested in more formal meditation. She trained with a Transcendental Meditation instructor and used times of solitude to develop her practice. Cecil Beaton believed that for Garbo nothing in life existed outside the present moment. Sam Green was also a devotee of Transcendental Meditation. Green always maintained that the reason Garbo stopped making movies was for her own personal development. She sought silence and solitude because she wanted to live a modest and healthy life away from the public eye. Ultimately, her devotion to her craft as an actor was outweighed by her desire for a purer existence of seclusion and tranquillity. That tranquillity would have been impossible if she had remained in Hollywood. In the end, her need to continue her inner journey of self-discovery was irresistible. In the 1940s, Garbo began to follow a natural-eating regime developed by the nutritionist and founder of the natural food movement, Gayelord Hauser. Hauser recommended people increase their intake of his 'wonder foods' which included brewer's yeast, powdered milk, wheatgerm and blackstrap molasses. Under his guidance, Garbo avoided flour and refined sugar. She become a regular visitor to health food stores. A wholefood diet became a lifelong interest.

In October 1938, she complained to reporters about their constant harassment during her trip with Leopold Stokowski. It did not feel like a holiday because she had not been left in peace. In early October 1951, Garbo agreed to dine at 10 Downing Street with the Prime Minister, Clement Attlee. The dinner took place just two weeks before the general election of 25 October, in which Attlee would narrowly lose to Winston Churchill. Garbo made a condition of her visit that it should be private, she would be unaccompanied, and there would be strictly no press coverage. The press could never forgive her for not playing along. They needed stories and photo opportunities to fill column inches. In the absence of real truths they concocted their own. The media storm that followed her death in 1990 featured reports on Garbo's lonely and bitter old age. These reports were pure fantasy. Garbo's psychologist Eric Drimmer maintained that she was not friendless and isolated but this idea had been invented by people who did not know her. She was undeniably antipathetic towards crowds but she had good reason.

During her childhood, there was no private space for quiet contemplation in the tiny apartment her family occupied in Södermalm. The young Greta Gustafsson had no choice but to retreat to a place of solitude constructed entirely in her mind. Later when she became wealthy, she was able to transform this internal solitary space into an external reality. She chose her home at 1717 San Vicente Boulevard because the house was well set back from the road, standing at the end of a long drive. It was a comfortable, three bedroom stucco house. Its only drawback was that it did not have a swimming pool. A keen swimmer, Garbo would get up at sunrise each day, take a short walk down to the deserted beach and lose herself in the immense blue emptiness of the sea.

You have a queer way of looking at things.

CLARK GABLE TO GARBO
SUSAN LENOX: HER FALL AND RISE
METRO-GOLDWYN-MAYER 1931

Self-actualised people are independent thinkers.

Joan Crawford once boasted that she never left the house unless she looked like 'Joan Crawford - The Movie Star'. Garbo did the opposite, making no effort at all to project the perfect image of 'Garbo' when out in public. On 18 October 1938, the American Coiffure Guild sent a formal complaint to Metro-Goldwyn-Mayer. They claimed that Garbo was damaging the hairdressing industry because she washed her hair herself and left it to dry naturally without styling it. Women across America were copying her and hairdressers were losing business. They declared Garbo's style 'wholly unsuitable' for the women of America and demanded that she change her look. Garbo refused. Her niece, the Columbia Law School graduate, Gray Reisfield, felt that a streak of unconventionality ran through everything Garbo did. Her dress sense, her lack of jewellery and make-up, her unfussy hairstyle were all expressions of her frank and straightforward individuality. She was a freethinker in a society straitjacketed by conformity. Garbo once told her friend Raymond Daum that she had always lived life in her own peculiar way as a 'free-going spirit'. She told him that she had to do this otherwise she could not exist.

As she became more self-actualised, she pushed at the edges of conventional society and she encouraged her friends to share in her sense of freedom. Wilhelm Sorensen, the son of a wealthy Swedish businessman, first met Garbo at a New Year's Eve party in Stockholm in 1928. She invited him to visit her in California and in September the following year, he took her up on her offer. Each day he drove her to

Metro-Goldwyn-Mayer where she was filming her last silent production *The Kiss*. They soon became 'friends with benefits'. He would join Garbo and Nils Asther to swim naked in her pool. Her neighbours' children would invite their friends to sit on the roof of the neighbouring house and spy on the three nude bathers. At a Christmas party in 1930, Garbo's reputation as an untamed spirit was cemented when she suggested that everyone strip naked and jump into the swimming pool. A decade later, Garbo's attitude to nudity had remained unchanged. In 1940, Raymond Daum's father was renting a property next to Gayelord Hauser's hideaway in Palm Springs. Daum's father complained about 'that skinny Swedish actress' always running around naked in the backyard.

When Garbo did put on clothes, her wardrobe was decidedly unconventional for the time. She described herself as having 'a distinctly trousered attitude to life'. She wore twill jackets, suits, tailored waistcoats, trench coats, cotton shirts and ties. She had a much-loved pair of brogues that she would wear for her solitary country walks. She wore men's slippers and silk dressing gowns around her home. In public, she saw no problem in wearing what was considered to be typically male attire. But in the 1920s and 1930s dressing in this way was regarded as transgressive and shocking. When Garbo and Mercedes de Acosta strolled along Hollywood Boulevard wearing trousers, scandalised journalists ran the headline: 'Garbo In Pants!' Several years later, Garbo rocked the establishment again when she arrived at the Monte Carlo Sporting Club in slacks. This contravened the casino's strict rule that ladies must wear dresses. Aristotle Onassis, the club's owner no less, intervened personally and an exception to the rule was made - the first in the club's history - so that Garbo could enter.

Garbo's future lover, Mercedes de Acosta, was raised ostensibly as a boy. She played games with boys and dressed in Eton suits. When she was sent away to a convent, Mercedes told the nuns that she did not consider herself male or female but something in between. The nuns' attempts to teach her to be 'more feminine' failed miserably and she ran away. Garbo, similarly, saw herself as neither male nor female but as primarily 'other'. Depending on her mood, she used male as well as female pronouns when talking about herself. She told Raymond Daum that she thought of herself not as man or woman but as mankind. To her the word 'girl' seemed diminutive. She preferred to use 'woman', 'man' or 'boy'. In many ways, Garbo lampooned society's fixation with gender labels. When she telephoned Mercedes to entice her away from a party given by the actress Pola Negri, Garbo used the pseudonym Mr Toscar. At a private dinner during the 1940 presidential election race, she suggested that her friends might like to vote for her. She said she was a fine man who could make a go of being President of the United States. Cecil Beaton asked Garbo to marry him on several occasions during their long friendship. When talking about his repeated marriage proposals, she called them his attempts to make an honest boy out of her. During the filming of *Ninotchka*, Ina Claire, Garbo's co-star, persuaded a stagehand to conceal her on set. She wanted to observe Garbo playing a particularly emotional scene. When she later complimented Garbo for her skill at producing genuine tears, Garbo described the ability as 'decidedly unmanly'. Sometimes Garbo would describe herself in both masculine and feminine terms in the same sentence. She told Sam Green that she was not only a kept woman but also a good man. Equally, Garbo played with gender when referring to her friends. On a trip to Switzerland in 1967, she asked Salka Viertel to be a good boy and meet her at the airport. She began letters to Baroness Cécile de Rothschild with the words, 'Warmest greetings, dear boy.' Garbo preferred to inhabit a space that lay beyond society's rigid gender norms. One of the many paintings she acquired as an art collector was *Enfant Assis En Robe Bleue / Child Seated In Blue Dress*. It was a portrait of Auguste Renoir's nephew Edmond painted by the artist in 1889. Renoir depicted the child with soft features and waist-length blond hair and it was this androgynous quality that prompted Garbo to purchase the painting.

In a number of her films, screenwriters depicted Garbo's characters as undermining heteronormative gender roles. In *Susan Lenox* she wears Clarke Gable's pyjamas and rides on the running board of his car. In *Flesh and the Devil,* she is the antithesis of passive submission. She is the seducer, ravishing John Gilbert with her kisses. He lays his head on her chest while she caresses him, an early reversal in 1920s Hollywood of orthodox gender roles . This theme continues in *A Woman Of Affairs* when she pulls John Gilbert close to her and grasps his face in her hands taking the assertive role in their on-screen kiss. In the same film her character, Diana Merrick, is described as a gallant gentleman with a gentleman's honour. These portrayals made certain powerful men at Metro-Goldwyn-Mayer decidedly uneasy. When Mercedes de Acosta wrote *Desperate* in 1931, a screenplay in which Garbo would be disguised as a boy, Metro-Goldwyn-Mayer producer Irving Thalberg was incensed. He rounded on Mercedes, telling her, 'We have been building Garbo up for years as a great glamorous actress, and now you come along and try to put her into pants and make a monkey out of her!'[13] He told her that all of America would turn against Garbo if she wore men's clothes in a film. Soon afterwards the project was dropped.

As a young woman at stage school in Stockholm, Garbo had a keen interest in playing male roles. She was particularly drawn to the male characters in the work of Russian playwrights such as Pushkin and Chekov. The idea of a woman dressing as a man, the idea of challenging gender conventions, thrilled her. During her film career Garbo expressed a desire to portray a variety of famous male characters on screen including Dorian Gray and Hamlet. Perhaps the closest she ever got to these ambitions was in the role of Queen Christina, a part she chose herself. Her autonomy was facilitated by a new contract with Metro-

Goldwyn-Mayer in 1933 that gave Garbo complete control over her choice of script and co-star. The real-life Queen Christina became ruler of Sweden in 1632. Her father, King Gustav II Adolf, was killed at the Battle of Lützen during the Thirty Years War. He had secured his daughter's right to inherit the throne despite her gender and had arranged for her to have the kind of education normally reserved for boys. Christina was an unconventional woman who rejected traditionally accepted gender roles. When she was sworn in at her coronation, she demanded the word 'king' be used instead of 'queen'. Unsurprisingly, Garbo was drawn to the strong convictions and unconventionality of the Swedish monarch. In *Queen Christina*, Garbo finally gets to wear trousers, albeit 17th-century ones. She spends the night at an inn disguised as a young man. She plans a romantic liaison with her lady-in-waiting, kissing her on the lips like a lover. The film was scripted by Salka Viertel. Four years later, Garbo told Viertel of her continued 'longing for trousers'. At the time, Viertel was working on another Garbo vehicle, *Marie Walewska* (Metro-Goldwyn-Mayer, 1937), a period drama based on the life of Napoleon Bonaparte's mistress. Garbo implored Viertel to write a scene that would enable her to wear trousers again. This was quickly vetoed by the film's producer, Bernie Hyman. The Hays Code had just been introduced, instigating film censorship based on strict moral guidelines. The Code was named after Republican Senator Will Hays who was the President of the Motion Picture

Association of America from 1922 to 1945. Under the direction of ultra-conservative Catholic Joseph Breen, the Breen Office was tasked with implementing the Hays Code. Breen had already voiced grave reservations about the adulterous nature of the relationship between Marie Walewska and Napoleon. Metro-Goldwyn-Mayer took great pains to reassure Breen that Marie became an adulteress only because she was forced to do so against her will. Hyman did not want to start another controversy by putting Garbo in trousers. As he put it, he didn't want to risk portraying Marie Walewska as a 'baritone babe'.

During the 1930s, the free-spirited Garbo would fall foul of the Hays Code on numerous occasions. In 1941, the Legion of Decency, a Catholic morality watchdog, denounced the Garbo movie *Two-Faced Woman* as an affront to public decency. Garbo's Karin Borg pretends to be her own fictitious twin sister in order to entrap her husband Larry who she suspects of being unfaithful. To the Legion of Decency the film made light of adultery. Scenes were added to mitigate the adulterous tone but this was not enough to satisfy the Legion and the film was banned in several cities across the United States. After a screening in Rhode Island, a furious group of Catholics besieged the local police station. The next day further showings of the film were prohibited.

Even before the advent of the Hays Code, Garbo's films pushed at the boundaries of conventional ideas of decency. In *A Woman of Affairs* Garbo's character, Diana Merrick, finds solace in a string of lovers after she is falsely accused of prompting her husband's suicide. In the opening scene of *Mata Hari*, Garbo performs a seductive dance. Her costume exposes her bare thighs and only breast plates cover her upper torso. She glides across the stage, caressing her body sensuously with her hands and gyrating her hips for the camera. This provoked horrified gasps from scandalised members of the audience at the film's premiere on 26 December 1931.

When it came to intimate relationships, Garbo flouted society's rigid conventions. She had many affairs and enjoyed the company of both male and female lovers. Along with John Gilbert, Sven Hugo Borg and Mercedes de Acosta, Garbo had romantic entanglements with the actors Louise Brooks, Mona Mårtensen and Vera Schmiterlow. As a young woman, she was also involved with her fellow drama student, Mimi Pollack, who later worked as an actor and theatre director. Much of their early correspondence reveals the romantic nature of their friendship. In a letter, written to Pollack much later in 1930, Garbo discloses her belief that the two of them had always belonged together. When Garbo first moved to New York in 1944, she frequented Valeska's Beggar Bar, a lesbian nightclub in Greenwich Village. The club was named after its owner, the German Jewish cabaret artist Valeska Gert, a recent refugee from Hitler's Germany. Here Garbo spent time with the American poet and activist Muriel Rukeyser and another Jewish refugee, the singer Marianne Oswald. Oswald, along with actresses Maria

Collm and Kadidja Wedekind, regularly entertained the Beggar Bar clientele, belting out cabaret numbers to an audience who sat on upturned crates and rested their drinks on beer barrels. Among her circle of friends, Garbo openly celebrated her own unorthodox approach to love. Every cabin on Aristotle Onassis' yacht was named after a Greek island. Whenever she was on board, Garbo waggishly chose the cabin named after the island of *Lesbos*. Many of Garbo's films also carried a strong homoerotic subtext. In *Flesh and the Devil* best friends Leo (John Gilbert) and Ulrich (Lars Hanson) often stare into each other's eyes with the intensity of lovers. This prompts Pastor Voss (George Fawcett) to remark that ever since they were boys he has never seen them apart. In *A Woman of Affairs,* Jeffrey Merrick (Douglas Fairbanks Jnr) is infatuated with David Furness (Johnny Mack Brown). When David dies, Jeffrey is devastated, more it seems than David's own wife Diana, played by Garbo.

Garbo's characters demonstrated an independence of thought that directly challenged the accepted patriarchal values of the time. In *Susan Lenox*, her father complains that she is too independent, reading novels and getting 'crazy notions' in her head. He has decided that she will marry their neighbour, a boorish alcoholic named Jeb Mondstrum (Alan Hale). She refuses and runs away. When her father and Mondstrum catch up with her, she defies them again, stealing their horse and cart to make her getaway. In *Anna Christie,* Anna has a suitor called Matt (Charles Bickford). Towards the end of the film, Matt says Anna will take orders from him now - her father has had his hold over her for long enough. Garbo's Anna rejects the entire system of patriarchal control, telling both Matt and her father she will please herself - no man can tell her what to do. In *Two-Faced Woman*, Larry (Melvin Douglas) orders his wife Karin (Garbo) to pack up her things and move to New York with him. In the America of the 1920s, a woman was expected to love, honour and obey her husband but Karin will not be given orders. She refuses to go and insists that they should be making decisions together. The suggestion that men and women should share decision taking bordered on revolution. In her personal life Garbo admired such famous feminists as George Sand and Gertrude Stein, even imitating Stein in her correspondence to Salka Viertel: 'Trousers, girls in trousers, pressed trousers, girls, trousers, trousers.'

Garbo questioned many ideas that others simply accepted. When it came to the notion of the American Dream, Garbo did not romanticise America as the land of opportunity. America was a place where too many people were caught up in the relentless pursuit of wealth. Garbo preferred the more humane, less ostentatious way of life of her friends and family back in Sweden. When Garbo was first summoned to America by Louis B. Mayer she was in no hurry to get there. Mayer expected her and Mauritz Stiller to sail for New York on 1 May 1925. They didn't set sail until two months later on 31 June. Mayer was infuriated by their insouciance. This was the beginning of the cat-and-mouse relationship between Garbo and one of the most formidable men in Hollywood. She told her housekeeper to say she was unavailable whenever Mayer phoned her at home. If Mayer insisted she show up at a certain time at the studio, she stayed away. When Mayer sent her threatening telegrams, she ignored them.

She was the first person to refuse an invitation to Pickfair, the legendary home of Douglas Fairbanks and Mary Pickford, Hollywood's most influential couple. She turned down three invitations to the White House from Jackie Kennedy until she was finally persuaded to visit in October 1963. She agreed on the condition that the gathering would be small and completely secret. Six people, including the President and the First Lady, gathered to have dinner with her. She jumped on Lincoln's bed during the White House tour. As a practical joke on the President's close friend Lem Billings, she pretended not to recall meeting him earlier in the year on the Italian Riviera. She was delighted that the President did not retire to his study after dinner as was usual but made an exception for Garbo, staying on with his guests. Garbo was openly critical of the fast pace of American life. During production of *The Temptress*, she observed that everybody seemed to be in a constant hurry, always running. People in Sweden did not rush about so.

Not to think, only to live, only to feel.

GARBO IN ANNA KARENINA
METRO-GOLDWYN-MAYER 1935

Self-actualised people are able to live fully in the present moment.

In *Romance*, Rita Cavallini (Garbo), tells her lover, Tom Armstrong (Gavin Gordon), that the future and the past are just clouds and shadows. The only thing of any substance is the little minute that we call 'today'. Garbo was careful not to lose sight of today in anticipation of tomorrow. Living in the vibrancy of the moment was what it meant to be fully alive. The playwright Kenneth Jupp first met Garbo in 1961 at a house party in the Manhattan home of actor Zachary Scott. Jupp was struck by her ability to focus completely on the present to the exclusion of all else. This quality had been noted before by the actor Judith Malina when she spied Garbo in a small confectioner's in Madison Avenue. Malina described Garbo's attention focused just as intensely on the person behind the counter as it would have been on any of her leading men. Garbo's reverence for the vitality of the moment was one reason she didn't rehearse her scenes before a take. She learned her lines at home, came into the studio and delivered them as the camera rolled.

The South American heartthrob Ramon Novarro starred opposite Garbo as her romantic interest, Lieutenant Alexis Rosanoff, in *Mata Hari*. Novarro was unnerved by her reluctance to rehearse until he saw the value in the immediacy of her approach. He observed Garbo's whole being change as the cameras turned over and the scene began. It was as if she took hold of the unfolding moment, generating an intensity that energised the actor playing opposite her. Her presence in linear time powered her presence on screen. Ramon Novarro tells Garbo's Mata

Hari that he expects the war to be over by the end of next year. 'I never look ahead,' she replies. In *Ninotchka*, she observes that nothing is permanent, all civilisations crumble. She says that we should take our time and have 'our moment'.

Garbo was walking on the beach in Santa Monica with Mercedes de Acosta when she recognised the beach house belonging to the director Ernst Lubitsch. She grabbed Mercedes' hand, marched up to the house and banged on the window. Lubitsch yelped, 'My God, Greta!' He took her in his arms and kissed her impetuously. Holding her hand, he told Garbo how much he had always wanted to direct her. She asked him to speak to the executives at Metro-Goldwyn-Mayer. Soon afterwards, he was announced as the director of Garbo's twenty-fifth Hollywood picture, *Ninotchka*. Released in 1939, it would become one of her most successful films.

Garbo was equally impetuous when she wanted advice about her growing art collection. Although she had never met him, she knew the actor Edward G. Robinson was a knowledgeable collector. With a painting under her arm, she went to his home and rang the door bell. When the door opened, she simply said, 'Is Mr. Robinson in? My name is Garbo.' Surprised to find the 'Great Garbo' on his doorstep, Robinson invited her in. The painting under her arm was a landscape by an unknown artist. Robinson advised her to hang the picture in her house so she could see it in different light at different times of day. When she told him the artist was down on his luck and needed the money, Robinson encouraged her to buy the picture regardless. She did. Garbo enjoyed a sensuous relationship with the world. When she first visited Berlin she immediately liked the city because of the way it smelled. This was how she entered into the richness of life - through its physical wonders. The taste of Coney Island hotdogs, the feel of torrential rain drumming on her skin, the popping of soap bubbles on water, all held Garbo captivated in the present moment. According to her friend Jane Perry Gunther, Garbo had held onto the ability to take a child-like delight in all things.

Garbo signed her first contract with Metro-Goldwyn-Mayer at the studio's Broadway office in 1926. Publicist Howard Dietz thought her rather eccentric as she drifted around smelling the walls and caressing the curtains. In response to Dietz's quizzical stare, she told him she was gaining a sense of the character of the room. This moment is famously re-imagined in *Queen Christina*. Stopping for the night at an inn, she glides around her bedroom stroking wall hangings, sideboards, candlesticks and jewellery boxes. In the same film, she tells the Lord Chancellor how much she loves snow. She describes it as being like the wild sea, something to lose oneself in. In *Camille*, she bends down to smell the earth during a walk in the countryside. She tells her lover, Armand, that it has a beautiful aroma like perfume. In *Two-Faced Woman*, she suggests that rolling about in the snow can be a purifying experience and in *Mata Hari*, she remarks on the beauty of Paris in the springtime with all its chestnut trees in blossom. The Cloisters Museum in New York has a permanent exhibition of the *Unicorn Tapestries*. The collection dates from the beginning of the 16th century and was purportedly commissioned for the marriage of the French king, Louis XII. It depicts a group of noblemen engaged in a hunt for a unicorn. Garbo visited the exhibition with Cecil Beaton in the spring of 1946. Beaton described her growing euphoria as she took in every detail of the seven tapestries on show. She whistled and sighed as she regarded the finely crafted butterflies and wildflowers woven into the delicate wall hangings. She told Beaton how incredible human beings were that they could create something of such beauty. Garbo was able to respond energetically to the stimuli she encountered. She was able to find enjoyment in revisiting a work of art again and again. She visited the Durlacher Brothers Gallery in Manhattan repeatedly to look at the symbol-rich paintings of the Russian artist Pavel Tchelitchew. By the 1940s, she had become an avid art collector. This prompted her friend, the composer David Diamond, to nickname her Midtown apartment 'Le Petit Musée'. Howard Dietz also collected art. He acknowledged Garbo as someone who could study a piece of art in great detail. He felt she contemplated artworks 'patiently'.

As Yvonne Valbret in *Inspiration*, she apologises to her ex-lover André that she has not wrapped his love letters neatly, ready for him to collect. Instead, she has been reading them over and over again, struck by how beautiful they are.

She puts a record on the gramophone and tells him she has played it again and again because it reminds her of the night he came back to her. Following the death of Mauritz Stiller, Garbo asked to see his possessions. She spent time touching items of particular significance: a rug she had seen him buy in Turkey, a suitcase he had bought in America. She lost herself in the memories evoked by these physical traces of their shared experiences. In later life, Garbo haunted the antique shops of Third Avenue. She would sit for hours in the workroom of one store in particular where craftsmen restored furniture. Without saying a word, she simply watched them work.

Garbo survived her years in Hollywood by taking long drives out to Lake Arrowhead. Surrounded by the wild beauty of lake and pine forest, she would sit quietly and read a book. In 1932, she planned six weeks of glorious isolation at Silver Lake in the Eastern Sierra. By the second day, she was so intoxicated with the intensity of the moment that she asked her chauffeur, James, to drive her back across the Mojave Desert to fetch Mercedes de Acosta. She wanted Mercedes to feel what she felt. There was always the risk that the break in her time at Silver Lake might rob her feeling of its initial intensity. But on her return with Mercedes, she re-experienced the landscape in all its glory as if seeing it for the first time. Mercedes likened Garbo to a nature spirit, formed out of rocks, storms, trees and water, jumping from rock to rock in her bare feet. For Christmas, Garbo bought Mercedes a raincoat, wellingtons and a sou'wester hat.

Whenever the weather turned stormy, she and Garbo would rush out to watch the lightning illuminate the sky and listen to the thunder crashing in the distance. Garbo was always exhilarated by the power of an electrical storm to inundate the senses. In *The Single Standard,* Garbo's character, Arden Stuart, tells her lover Packy Cannon (Nils Asther) how much she adores the pouring rain. In *Ninotchka*, Count Léon (Melvyn Douglas) asks Garbo's Ninotchka, 'Do Russians ever think about life, about the moment in which we are living? The only moment we ever really have.'

Happiness you cannot imagine. Happiness you must feel.

GARBO IN QUEEN CHRISTINA
METRO-GOLDWYN-MAYER 1933

Self-actualised people have more peak experiences more often.

Abraham Maslow was a revolutionary in the field of psychology. He produced his most groundbreaking work during the 1950s and 1960s, and his findings had profound implications for the future of psychotherapy. His approach extended beyond addressing what was wrong with a patient. He focused on what was right with the patient and how he or she could improve their psychological well-being further. One of the most extraordinary discoveries from Maslow's research was the phenomenon of 'peak experiences' - moments of rapture, described by his test subjects, where all sense of separateness from the world disappeared. Maslow believed that the degree of an individual's self-actualisation was proportionate to the frequency of peak experiences. Roberto Assagioli called peak experiences those feelings of positivity, illumination and joy that every human being is capable of having. The philosopher Colin Wilson was a proponent of Maslow's ideas and wrote extensively about the peak experience. Wilson championed a new kind of Romanticism that was, at its heart, a positive existentialism. He described the peak experience as a kind of flow experience, free from stagnation or boredom, where one feels truly alive.

Garbo had peak experiences from an early age. The young Greta Gustafsson was drawn to the theatre as an escape from the abject poverty of life in the slums of Södermalm. Her dreams of one day becoming an actress provided the stimulus for her frequent peak experiences. Working as a barber shop lather girl, Greta would spontaneously overflow with exuberance for no apparent reason. She would hug the proprietor's wife, saying one day she hoped to become a great actress. She would pirouette and laugh while cleaning the razors. When asked why she was laughing, she replied, 'Why isn't everyone laughing?' Greta spent many hours loitering at the stage doors of the Södra Theatre in Mosebacke Square. She saw her first play at the age of eleven. She said it felt like the gates of heaven were opening. Just six years later she was accepted into Stockholm's Royal Dramatic Academy. On receiving her acceptance letter, Greta's euphoria was so intense she thought she might die. It was arguably this intensity of feeling and devotion that powered her consummate artistry. Her intense commitment enabled her to enter fully into each character she portrayed. The journalist Sven Broman noted how completely she surrendered to this unitary experience. Garbo did not play Camille, Queen Christina or Anna Karenina. She was Camille, she was Queen Christina, she was Anna Karenina. Her oneness with a character unfolded purely in itself and for itself. She was transported. Colin Wilson described a similar experience when writing a book about the playwright George Bernard Shaw. As he wrote about Shaw's first big break, Wilson felt a sudden and intense joyfulness. It was as if he had become Shaw, as if he were living Shaw's original experience. This is what the philosopher Alfred North Whitehead described as the 'absoluteness of self-enjoyment'. It is the *aha!* moment of the peak experience. In the summer of 1975, Garbo stayed with

Carl and Kerstin Bernadotte at their country estate in Bastad, southern Sweden. One day at the local farm, she was fortunate enough to witness the birth of a calf. She was overcome with sudden feelings of elation and called out that she wished she had a camera. Garbo had spent most of her life avoiding cameras and this was the first time, her friend Kerstin noted, that she had ever asked for one, so intense was the wave of euphoria. Sailing across the Atlantic, she was overwhelmed by a precipitous happiness whenever she caught sight of the boundless sea. Arriving at Silver Lake with Mercedes de Acosta, she was instantly euphoric even though she had been there only the day before. Walking in the mountains, Cecil Beaton described her as the most affable companion, joyously reciting poetry and singing songs. Garbo admitted she regularly walked for miles on her own. Immersed in a joyful connection with the wild, all feelings of separateness from the universe disappeared. She would talk to herself, sing and shout out loud.

A notable aspect of the peak experience is the ability to see commonplace things as if for the first time. Colin Wilson described this as the lowering of the indifference threshold. In *Romance* Garbo's character, Rita Cavallini, reminds her benefactor, Cornelius van Tuyl (Lewis Stone) of the night he stood beneath her window and she sang Schubert to him. She remembers how all the roses in the world seemed to blossom in the moonlight 'and the wind and the sea and the big old moon'. The critic Kenneth Tynan believed fame had insulated Garbo from everyday experiences. What was mundane to many people was perceived as unusual or rare by Garbo. In effect, her celebrity had made her more susceptible to peak experiences. A walk down a busy street became a semi-mystical adventure. Publicist Hubert Voight once took her to dine at the home of Lawrence Tibbett, the celebrated American baritone. As Tibbett sang for her, she was swept away in the moment and began to join in. Voight described her in that instant as the most beautiful creature he had ever seen, a child of the sun, shining with life.

Abraham Maslow maintained that peak experiences were responses to a sudden and profound sense of aliveness. He did not think they could be induced at will. Colin Wilson disagreed. Wilson felt that peak experiences could be actively induced using thought and imagination to focus the mind in a determined way. When students were asked to recall past experiences of intense good feeling, they started to have more peak experiences as a consequence. It was as if recalling previous peaks readied the mind for more. Garbo once remarked that the memory of her acceptance into the Royal Dramatic Academy could still induce, years later, the original euphoric feelings. These feelings were often so powerful that she found herself unable to breathe all over again. As children, Greta and her friend Elizabeth Malcolm would climb onto the roof of the outside toilet behind Greta's apartment building. There they would concentrate their imaginative powers on the idea of a beach, the sea and gentle music. They were able to induce in themselves the feeling of sitting on a beautiful beach with an orchestra playing in the distance. They could transport themselves away from the squalor of their surroundings at will, inducing sublime feelings of expansiveness and possibility. In *Queen Christina*, Christina and Don Antonio share a room at an inn, becoming lovers. She tells him she has memorised every inch of the room so she can relive the same beautiful experience in the future. In *Inspiration*, Garbo's Yvonne tells her lover Andre she intends to think only about the places they have been happy together. She wants to keep them in her memory and revisit them at will. 'Peakers' was the name Colin Wilson used to describe people who regularly had peak experiences. Wilson's close friend, a musician, confided how he was often radically affected by a piece of music. He would come home, pour himself a whisky and listen to a record. He described listening to a suite of dances by Pretorius and feeling a potent spiritual communion, almost as if he had become the music. Similarly, in *Mata Hari*, Garbo has the line: 'My mind is so far away when I dance, I live in another age.' Through the exotic beauty of her Javanese dance, she is transfigured. She becomes a different being in a different time. Many of Garbo's characters appear to be peakers. Queen Christina, Yvonne Valbret, Rita Cavallini, Mata Hari all display moments of intense aliveness where fear and weakness fall away. In life Garbo experienced moments of profound wonder at the most mundane, everyday things. At these moments, all separateness and distance from the outside world evaporated. Pure happiness consumed her. Garbo once showed Mercedes de Acosta her favourite tree.

It stood lifeless and unremarkable outside Garbo's bedroom window. Whenever she was tired of Hollywood and wanted to feel uplifted, Garbo would look at the tree. She would imagine herself back in Sweden. She would imagine that the winter had made the tree leafless and soon snow would come to rest on its branches. She told Mercedes that the tree was her joy. She called it her 'winter tree'.

She is rather a crazy mystic Swede.

MERCEDES DE ACOSTA ON GARBO

Self-actualised people see their own interconnectedness with the rest of the cosmos.

'What do you believe about god?' was a question Garbo often asked people she met. A devout Christian or a committed atheist might ask, 'Do you believe in God?' But Garbo was not looking for a simple 'yes' or 'no'. She phrased her inquiry as an open question because she was open to a multiplicity of answers and possibilities. Cecil Beaton called her an enigma brimming with spiritual thoughts. Leif Erickson, her co-star in *Marie Walewska*, described her as the hippie of the world, surveying the scene but not partaking in it. She was in the world but not of the world. Mercedes de Acosta described her as a kind of wild mystic. Mercedes saw in Garbo a profound soul quality that seemed to lift her beyond the material world. Like Garbo, Mercedes was curious about the possibilities of spiratal development. She was a devotee of the Indian sages Ramana Maharshi and Sri Meher Baba. She practised yoga, dabbled in astrology and was a friend of the poet Kahlil Gibran who introduced her to the Hindu texts *The Bhagavad Gita*, *The Mahabharata* and *The Upanishads*. Mercedes had extrasensory abilities that had begun to develop when she was very young. She sensed there were powerful psychic forces at work in her relationship with Garbo; the deep affection the two women shared had opened a metaphysical channel between them.

Mercedes believed Garbo so captivated the public because her performances radiated a celestial quality. According to Mercedes, someone watching Garbo on screen came into contact with mystic forces that were incomprehensible. Mauritz Stiller pictured the ideal woman as super sensual, spiritual and mystic. These were the qualities he was looking for in a protégé and Garbo was all these things. Her other-worldliness is depicted in her films over and over again. Her Javanese temple dance bewitches the opening frames of *Mata Hari*. In *Camille,* she tells Armand's father of her premonition of death. In *Anna Christie,* she intimates knowledge of after-death states and reincarnation. She describes being lost in a fog for what seems like forever, ultimately emerging with no memory of what happened before. Perhaps this was what Mercedes first saw when she described Garbo's eyes as having a look of eternity.

For Garbo, belief in a superlunary consciousness provided an anchor in an uncertain world. With unshakeable faith came surety, protection and a sense of belonging. Yet her spiritual inclination did not take her in the direction of organised religion. She believed there was great wisdom in the Bible but found the Church's literal interpretation asinine. Her friendship with Mercedes brought her into contact with a hidden world of occult beliefs and hermetic theology. She came to realise there was an esoteric meaning to the Bible that guided the reader away from crude ideas of hellfire and damnation. This arcane exegesis revealed a path of goodness, which Garbo described as the greatest force in the world. Christianity, like all world religions, formed an integral part of a much greater whole, but it did not provide the complete picture. There was a hidden truth known to students of ancient mystery traditions which revealed the secrets of the cosmos. One night, on a mountain peak in California's Casa del Mare, Mercedes initiated Garbo into the ideas of the esoteric movement called Theosophy. In 1875, the Russian occultist Helena Petrovna Blavatsky, her companion Henry Steele Olcott and the esotericist William Quan Judge founded the Theosophical Society. Many of its doctrines were inspired by Blavatsky's travels in India and Tibet. The term 'Theosophy' means literally 'divine wisdom'. The Theosophical Society aimed to form a nucleus of universal brotherhood amongst all people regardless of the differences between them. It promoted the comparative study of religion, philosophy and science. It advocated the investigation of unexplained natural laws and the latent powers hidden within humanity. On that mountaintop in Casa del Mare, Garbo and Mercedes spent the entire night talking about occult cosmology or sitting in silent contemplation. Mercedes later likened Garbo to the physical embodiment of an elemental goddess, an idea redolent of the Theosophical doctrine that humankind is descended from the divine.

Years after the two women's mountaintop vigil, Garbo met Leopold Stokowski for the first time at a party given by the novelist, Anita Loos. A committed occultist, Stokowski told Garbo they shared a destiny that had been written in the stars by the gods themselves. Stokowski shared with her esoteric knowledge he had gained during his travels in India. He fascinated Garbo with his description of a whole day spent on a mountaintop discussing destiny and the soul with an Indian sage. It was only after he and the sage had parted that Stokowski realised they had understood each other perfectly - even though he spoke no Hindi and the sage spoke no English. Stokowski's story inevitably reminded Garbo of her earlier mountaintop vigil with Mercedes de Acosta. In that incarnation of the story, the place of the sage had been taken by Mercedes and Stokowski's role as initiate had been played by Garbo.

With Sam Green, Garbo would often discuss spiritual questions ranging from metempsychosis to mediumship and communication with spirits. In *The Painted Veil*, Garbo's character, Katrin, declares her love for China. Soon after arriving in that country, she describes it as so full of spells, they seem to be the reason for everything. She attends a Chinese sun and moon festival. Performers in ornate costumes act out a legend in which the sun god slays a dragon to save his lover so they can roam the skies for all eternity. She has her fortune told in a Buddhist temple, heady with burning incense and said to be inhabited by mighty gods. Garbo portrays Katrin as an earnest spiritual seeker with a yearning to experience the ancient spirituality of China, a desire Garbo shared.

In a letter to Garbo, dated 3 November 1957, Cecil Beaton told her he had noticed her spiritual thoughts turning towards the Orient. Garbo's fascination with eastern philosophies and mystical traditions was strongly influenced by her relationship with Mercedes. In many ways Mercedes was her spiritual mentor. In 1933, Mercedes suffered serious injuries in a traffic accident. She was taking an afternoon drive in the San Fernando Valley when she was involved in a collision at a crossroads. She was thrown from her car and struck her head on the roadway. She was rushed to Santa Monica Hospital in a critical condition. Unconscious, between life and death, she had the impression that her spirit had travelled great distances from her body. Later she was told she had been unconscious barely a few moments. Following her convalescence, Mercedes suffered periods of depression and even contemplated suicide. Help came in the form of Sri Meher Baba. He told her that suicide would simply result in another incarnation involving the same problems. The only answer was to develop God Realisation, to see the divine in everything. If Mercedes did this, he advised, everything would become easier.

Mercedes met the author Paul Brunton at the home of Garbo's costume designer, Adrian. In Brunton's book, *A Search in Secret India*, Mercedes learned about Ramana Maharshi. Maharshi believed that silence and self-enquiry were the surest routes to self-realisation. He saw the Self as a non-personal, all inclusive awareness from which everything manifested. In the autumn of 1936, Sri Meher Baba invited her to visit him in Cannes on the French Riviera. She travelled to France and spent a short time as his pupil. Garbo was the only person who knew where she had gone. Before Mercedes left him, Baba told her she must always keep moving. That was the point of life, never to become static. Two years later, in October 1938, Mercedes began her six month odyssey in India. She visited Jaipur and the Taj Mahal and saw Sri Meher Baba once more. She was also granted an audience with Ramana Maharshi, a mystic she had previously only read about. He told her that she was to become an adept. He told her she must seek the Self within the Spiritual Heart. Shortly afterwards she sailed back to America via Colombo and Bombay. Her experiences in India had had a profound effect on her. She became so immersed in the eastern tradition that she planned one day to write a thesis on Indian philosophy. Sadly, she died before she could complete the task.

Garbo had rejected the organised religion of the Christian church for more heterodox spiritual beliefs. She regarded many devout Christians as hypocritical. The dress designer Valentina Schlee had once been a close friend. When Valentina's husband George began spending more time with Garbo, Valentina was consumed with resentment and hatred. When Schlee died, Valentina barred Garbo from attending his funeral. She arranged for a priest to exorcise every room in their home that might bear traces of her. Garbo, who had done nothing wrong, was stung by Valentina's actions. It was incredible to her that a former friend and committed Christian could behave with such heartless malice towards another human being. In Christianity's place, Garbo found Theosophy, an altogether more inclusive spiritual tradition. Its occult aspects captured her imagination. She was drawn to the concepts of astral travel, humanity's divine origins, reincarnation and the rejection of materialism, all ideas to be found in the writings of Helena Blavatsky. Garbo's nonconformist tendencies led her to the unorthodox figure of Blavatsky for inspiration. James Pope-Hennessy, the travel writer and friend of Cecil Beaton, was quick to notice Garbo's predilection for this eastward-looking spiritual movement. In a letter, he described Garbo as 'interested in Theosophy, dieting, and all other cranky subjects.'

In *Camille* Garbo makes the emphatic statement, 'I don't like sad thoughts!' Fifty-one years later, Sven Broman and his wife found Garbo reading a guide to the Law of Attraction when they visited her apartment in the winter of 1987. Garbo's interest in metaphysics and the occult was sustained by Mercedes, acting as her mentor and a small coterie of like-minded people. Towards the end of 1919, Mercedes had read Blavatsky's ambitious, seminal work, *The Secret Doctrine*. She saw it as an indispensable introduction for any spiritual novice seeking the truth. She read *The Tibetan Book of the Dead* and investigated the Theosophical concepts of astral travel and reincarnation. The sheer scale of *The Secret Doctrine* consolidated her interest in the Theosophical movement and she began to apply its principles to her own life. She became close friends with the American dancer Isadora Duncan, regarded as the mother of modern dance. Duncan's innovative performances traced dance to its ancient roots as a sacred art. Elemental power inspired her modernist choreography. Her style evoked a deep communion with nature, her movements reflecting the vitality of the waves rising and falling in the ocean or the trees bending in the wind. Duncan once said that each incarnation held within it a spiritual line, an upward curve towards the divine. This idea had been earlier expressed by the Theosophical author C. Jinarajadasa. He described man as an immortal soul growing through the ages on a road to perfection. With each evolutionary cycle, the human spirit would become ever more refined, until, eventually man would return to the godhead. This is a central tenet of Theosophical thought. Mercedes became friends with the notable Theosophist, Eleanor S. Cooley. Born in Liverpool in 1886, Cooley later moved to the US where she helped found Theosophical lodges in Cleveland, Ohio and New York City. Cooley was a student of Jiddu Krishnamurti, the leader of the Theosophical Society's Order of the Star in the East or OSE. For a long time it was anticipated that Krishnamurti would become a new world teacher, and the spiritual leader of the worldwide Theosophical movement. He was expected to show the world the one true path to enlightenment. On 3 August 1929, he made a now famous speech at Ommen in the Netherlands. He told the crowd that there was no one truth, no one way to enlightenment. Everybody had to discover their own path. On the same day, he dissolved the OSE and advocated that his followers begin their own search for meaning. He remained a world-renowned spiritual teacher and in the early 1940s Mercedes heard him speak many times. She saw him at Aldous

Huxley's home and sometimes at his own home in California's Ojai Valley. Krishnamurti became a friend and teacher, someone who Mercedes would call upon for advice. For Mercedes, he represented another side of California life, a more authentic side devoted to spiritual enlightenment through true metaphysical teachings. She once remarked that although scientists had split the atom in the physical world, Krishnamurti had split the core of thought in the spiritual world.

Garbo met Krishnamurti when she and Salka Viertel attended an autumn picnic party at the Huxleys' home in Tujunga Canyon in 1939. The guest list included many notable intellectuals, amongst them, the philosopher Bertrand Russell and the author Christopher Isherwood. Garbo had been eager to meet Krishnamurti for a long time and wanted to learn all she could from the former Theosophical guru. Typically, she arrived for her meeting with the great world teacher wearing her straw gardening hat and slacks.

Like Mercedes, Garbo assimilated Theosophical ideas into her own world view. In December 1936 she wrote to Hörke Wachtmeister telling her she believed in the absolute unity of the cosmos. She told Hörke of her conviction that everything was created from one spiritual essence, that we are all one. Shortly afterwards, she wrote to Hörke again, describing her aspiration to travel to India to find enlightenment. She returned to this theme in her correspondence with Salka Viertel. In a letter written from

Sweden in 1938, Garbo describes her desire to seek out 'beings' who could teach her a new way of living. She may well have been referring to Theosophy's mahatmas or masters of wisdom, human beings who had attained perfection through inward spiritual endeavour. Garbo's spiritual thirst prompted her to contemplate ending her film career and embarking on an odyssey to find these enlightened teachers.

In 1939's *Ninotchka*, she describes herself as just a small cog in the great wheel of evolution, a veiled reference to the Theosophical concept of involution and evolution. In Theosophical teaching, humanity's evolution begins when spirit infuses the physical world. Theosophy describes this as the involution of spirit into matter. Cyclical transmutations follow, enabling humanity to become finer and finer, ultimately evolving beyond the physical and returning to the divine. Garbo's interest in the occult led her to adopt a semi-ascetic lifestyle. When not working, she rose at 6am each day to practise yoga and perform breathing exercises. Well into her sixties, she practised callisthenics and headstands on the terrace of her apartment in Klosters. She rationed her intake of alcohol, at one time confessing she had owned the same bottle of Glögg for many years. She ate a largely vegetarian diet including plenty of vegetables, nuts and yoghurt following the advice of healthy eating guru Gayelord Hauser. Hauser believed a person could give up a favourite food for no more than three weeks at a time so he advocated reduction rather than abstinence. During the filming of

Marie Walewska, the sound technician detected unusual noise interference in the studio. Try as he might, he couldn't identify the strange sound or its source. On further investigation, and with the help of director Clarence Brown, he discovered the sound was coming from Garbo's dressing room where she was pureeing vegetables in a blender to make broth for lunch.

Garbo thought it important to remain unattached to material possessions. 'We all become slaves to our possessions... You should be able to look at what you have, stare at it there when you want to, and if it goes, it goes. That's that.'[14] As Mercedes wrote in her memoir, *Here Lies the Heart*, Garbo lived not just a solitary life but a simple and austere one as well. Cecil Beaton admired her spiritual diligence. He described her as a true ascetic, a crusader and spartan warrior whose mind was occupied only with the more uncorrupted aspects of life. The novelist Sinclair Lewis observed that of all the Hollywood actors he had known, she was the one who had never 'gone Hollywood'. Despite her commitment to a simple, frugal life, there was one decidedly non-ascetic pleasure that she could not deny herself. In 1939, Mercedes read an article by Mahatma Gandhi. He wrote that nicotine thickened the spiritual body and hampered its development. Mercedes immediately gave up smoking. Garbo did not.

When Garbo and Mercedes first met at Salka Viertel's house, in the summer of 1931, Mercedes felt they had met before. As she took Garbo's hand in hers, a sixth sense told

her they had known each other in many previous
incarnations. The idea of reincarnation is central to
Theosophical thought. Theosophy describes a wheel of
rebirths. Each living being is the product of many previous
lives all blended into one. Each new incarnation is strongly
influenced by the previous ones. Even in her youth, Garbo
thought that the soul did not die but went on a journey after
it left the body. When her father died on 20 June 1920, she
felt certain that he was extant in some form of after-death
state. In Greta's mind, he had simply gone somewhere else
where she was unable to see or to find him. Garbo was also
convinced that she had lived other lives. Travelling to Berlin,
in 1924, for the premiere of *Gösta Berlings Saga*, she had the
strangest sense that she was able to smell the city long before
she got there. What's more, the city's smell was hauntingly
familiar to her even though she had never visited before. She
realised she must have lived in the German capital in a
previous life. She discussed reincarnation with Sam Green
who was also a believer. He had studied the history of
reincarnation in different religious and spiritual systems.
Garbo and Green both read *Far Memory*, the autobiography
of the English novelist Joan Grant. She claimed to have the
gift of 'far memory' or the unusual ability to remember her
previous incarnations. For her, she maintained, the 'veil
between worlds' did not exist. Garbo and Green debated the
link between reincarnation and karma. Green proposed that
people were reincarnated according to their karma and
dependent on the lessons their spirits needed to learn in their

next lives. Garbo asked, if people found themselves living lives they didn't want, was it because of mistakes made in their previous incarnations? She joked that she would like to be reincarnated next in China because the Chinese did not get wrinkles. She wondered at the possibility of other worlds and other levels of existence beyond the material. She described being under ether in a hospital in California. She thought she discovered eternity but eternity was not for human beings to understand and, therefore, she had discovered nothing.

The incomprehensible nature of the divine was a recurring source of fascination for Garbo. She saw human beings as limited by the capacities of the human mind and never able to grasp the true nature of the infinite. The question was simply too big for them. Gnosis in its purest sense - knowledge of the divine - eluded Garbo. The occult author Gary Lachman described gnosis as 'the true, eternal and living reality'[15] and it was this ineffable reality that remained forever just beyond Garbo's reach. In *Queen Christina*, Don Antonio (John Gilbert) tells Garbo he perceives a mystery within her. She replies, revealingly, 'Is there not in every human being?'

Garbo may have been confounded in her attempts to experience eternity but she was not deterred from exploring other aspects of metaphysics. She was compelled by the idea that the human mind had the power to affect the material world. Throughout her life she held firm to the belief that goodness was the force with the greatest agency. With

Mercedes' help, she came to understand how thought could influence the sum total of good in the world.

In the months before her car accident, Mercedes had been tormented by profound feelings of melancholy. The trauma that followed the collision had a life-changing effect on her. She came to believe that the accident was the result of occult forces responding to her negative state of mind. She was struck by the realisation that a thought for good or ill had great power when combined with strong emotion. Her intense feelings for Garbo, she realised, were the causal agent that had led to their eventual meeting. When *Torrent* was released in February 1926, Mercedes saw the film at the Capitol Theatre in New York. She was so enraptured by Garbo she simply stayed in her seat to watch the film a second time. In the years that followed, she thought often about the enigmatic figure of Garbo and fantasised about meeting her one day in the flesh. Mercedes went on to become a successful playwright, eventually being contracted by RKO to pen a screenplay for Pola Negri. Before travelling to Hollywood to start work in June 1931, she took a holiday on Long Island with a small group of friends including the actress Tallulah Bankhead. One evening, Tallulah produced a pack of cards, claiming she had the gift of divination. She invited Mercedes to draw a card and make a wish. Mercedes, of course, silently wished to meet Greta Garbo. Tallulah then asked her to return the card to the pack. With suitable ceremony, Bankhead scanned the cards and made her divinatory pronouncement: Mercedes' wish would come true exactly three days after her arrival in Hollywood. On her third day in LA, Mercedes was invited to Salka Viertel's house for tea. She arrived promptly, keen to meet fellow writers and to make new friends in Hollywood. Salka told her they were just waiting for one more guest and moments later, Garbo appeared.

Garbo and Mercedes became interested in astral travel, a latent human power according to Theosophical tradition. Theosophy taught that adepts in the Far East had the ability to project their bodies at will onto the astral plane. Mercedes wanted to understand how they were able to pass consciously between material and immaterial worlds. She was a subscriber to the Theosophical belief that the soul travelled on the astral plane both during dreams and after death. In April 1949, she was living in an apartment at 5 Quai Voltaire in Paris with her friend Poppy Kirk. The concierge at the apartment building was a frail woman who had been ill for a long time. Mercedes visited her often to try to lift her spirits but, sadly, the ailing concierge died during Mercedes' stay in Paris. Shortly after her death, Mercedes perceived her astral body standing in the communal hallway.

Garbo was staying in Stockholm when Mercedes made the conscious attempt to project her body astrally from her home in Brentwood to Garbo's hotel room. On her astral visit, she took in the details of the room's colours, furnishings and decoration. When she later checked these details with Garbo, they matched the physical reality of the room exactly. The two women were certain that Mercedes was able to travel across the astral plane because powerful psychic forces connected them. Garbo believed astral connection was possible between people with a strong emotional bond. She told Hörke Wachtmeister she believed she could pop into Hörke's mind whenever she liked simply by concentrating. When Anna's affair with Count Vronsky comes to light in *Anna Karenina*, her scandalised husband banishes her from their home, telling their son, Sergei, she is dead. Sergei refuses to believe this. He suggests he and his mother will meet on the astral plane: 'If I go to sleep, I know mother will come and kiss me goodnight.'

In a letter dated 18 December 1972, Garbo told Salka Viertel, 'Let us not underestimate dreams! Someone sent me a magazine which had pages about dreams. Then I dreamed that a cat bit me. I looked it up just for the deviltry of it - it promised troubles to come and I got them. It's a good thing we don't remember dreams too often.'

Garbo felt building churches was a waste of money. Everything a person needed to connect with the divine was inside him or her already. Humankind was born to be connected with nature and all creation, to walk on grass, not asphalt. In the summer of 1949, Garbo and Cecil Beaton visited Lady Diana Cooper's chateau in Chantilly. Beaton noted Garbo's delight in the wild animals, the clear water and great avenues of trees. Garbo told him she wanted to lie and roll in the corn. On her many walks with Sam Green in 1970s New York, she often suggested they walk barefoot on the grass in Central Park. Whenever she saw a tree she liked, she would throw her arms around its trunk. Mercedes believed Garbo had an almost mystical relationship with the natural world which enabled her to exert a direct influence over her immediate surroundings. Whenever they went hiking in the mountains, there was brilliant sunshine every day. At night, the lake glowed in the moonlight and the mountain peaks glistered like crystal. Mercedes felt that nature was Garbo's element. It was a shame, she said, that Garbo had not yet had an opportunity to express that truth on film. Garbo told Beaton that closeness to nature was good for the spirit. She said it was possible to live in California, close to nature, and avoid being press-ganged into the Hollywood circus.

The philosopher Ken Wilber coined the term 'kosmocentric'. A kosmocentric thinker's perspective is centred in the unity of the cosmos, in the Whole or the Spirit. Garbo displayed this attitude to the world and it enabled her to experience what Roberto Assagioli described as 'a sense of elation, of expansion of consciousness, a sense of reverence, sometimes even of worship and joyous participation in that larger reality, a sense of relief from the narrow limitations of the personal self, and a sharing, a communion in universal life.'[16] A singular kosmocentric thinker, Garbo regularly practised her oneness with creation by doing her gardening in the nude.

Garbo saw herself as part of an interdependent human consciousness, not above or greater than anyone else but equal and connected. To a great extent, this explains her modesty about her talent as an actress and her position in Hollywood. She saw the world as one entity, not as a disparate collection of nations of which the United States was the preferable choice. When she arrived in Sweden on holiday, she told reporters she was glad to be home. She regarded America as a place like any other; one had good times there and one had bad times. Even in childhood, she imagined a world where people of all nations united as one in friendship and peace. The young Greta would perform for people queueing in Stockholm's soup kitchens. She would appear draped in white bedsheets as the Goddess of Peace and recite pacifist poems and speeches. Like many self-actualised people, Garbo's view of the world was not shaped by national or cultural boundaries.

When she found herself stranded in Berlin with co-star Einar Hanson (courtesy of Mauritz Stiller's stalled production of *The Odalisque From Smolna*) she immersed herself in the sights and the sounds of the city's alternative culture. From gay and lesbian nightclubs to international cinema and Josephine Baker's *La Revue Nègre*, she and Hanson took in the full panoply of the city's multicultural delights. Garbo loved speaking German and often spoke to Salka Viertel in an idiosyncratic English peppered with her favourite German words. Her literary tastes spanned continents. She read Dostoyevsky, Turgenev, Goethe, Brontë and Hemingway, and was the inspiration for the character of Elisabeth in Jean Cocteau's 1929 novel *Les Enfants Terribles*. Openness to the world and the crossing of cultural boundaries is a recurring motif in Garbo's films. In *Susan Lenox*, Garbo as Lenox joins the circus. There she is given the role of the 'Belle Fatima', a favourite of the Sultan of Turkey in a sideshow entitled 'The Beauties of All Nations'. In *The Painted Veil* she tells her co-star Herbert Marshall that she loves China, America and all the places she hasn't yet been. In *Wild Orchids* she embraces Javanese customs eagerly, sitting cross-legged on the floor to try the exotic dishes of a traditional Javanese banquet, something her husband (Lewis Stone) is far less keen to do.

Garbo explored those questions to which the Church seemed unable to provide satisfactory answers. Despite her reputation, Garbo was not a recluse. She told Raymond Daum that she could never spend a whole twenty-four hours alone in her apartment. She needed to be out in the world, to walk under the sky, to commune with the life around her. Mercedes de Acosta, her companion on her spiritual journey, believed it to be insurmountably difficult for artists to become spiritually developed because they could not jettison their egos and embrace detachment. Perhaps, in Garbo, she had found the one exception.

What's important is that whenever you meet your fellow man, you're kind and you're decent.

GARBO FROM WALKING WITH GARBO
A MEMOIR BY RAYMOND DAUM

Self-actualised people have a well-developed sense of compassion.

Garbo's cameraman, William Daniels, described her as someone who had the most beautiful feeling for people and for life. Garbo told Raymond Daum the most important thing in life was to be a decent human being, 'That's what counts, because if there aren't such people, then there's no hope for the world... The only thing you have is the fundamental thing inside you, whether you take it into a monastery or onto a soapbox.'[17] She felt deep concern for the suffering of others and was outraged when people were mistreated. Her friend and mentor Mauritz Stiller had delivered into Louis B. Mayer's hands the studio's greatest asset: Garbo. Yet Mayer cast him adrift. Stiller was unable to find work and was forced to return to Sweden a defeated and broken man.

When he died in Stockholm on 8 November 1928, Garbo was inconsolable. Though she was working on *Wild Orchids*, directed by Sidney Franklin, she begged Mayer to allow her time off to grieve Stiller's death. Mayer refused. It was only after shooting wrapped at the end of December that she was able to leave for Stockholm to visit Stiller's grave. En route for New York to board the MS Kungsholm, Garbo received a cable from Mayer demanding she return to Hollywood for retakes. Garbo ignored him.

She later told the playwright and columnist S. N. Behrman that she hated Mayer, not because of the way he had treated her but the way he had treated people she cared for. Her fellow Swede, Einar Hanson, also suffered at the hands of the Hollywood studio system. He appeared in a number of successful films including *Her Big Night* (Universal Jewel, 1926) and *The Masked Woman* (First National Pictures, 1927). As his fame grew, the studios pressured Hanson to conceal the fact that he was gay. Hanson found this deception incredibly difficult to sustain. On 3 June 1927, he and Garbo attended a small gathering at the Miramar Hotel. Hanson drank heavily all evening. Garbo pleaded with him not to drive home that night but to stay at hers. He refused. Several hours later he was found, barely alive, in the wreckage of his car. He died soon afterwards at the Santa Monica Hospital. Garbo was appalled by the way the studios had bullied him because of his homosexuality. She felt certain he would have been treated with more respect in Sweden. For a time, she withdrew into her own private world and considered leaving Hollywood once and for all. At stage school she had felt tremendous compassion for any student rebuked by a teacher, regardless of the reason. Students held back after class would later encounter Greta in the corridor, flinging her arms around them consolingly. To Garbo, people were basically the same. Everybody was born and grew up, everybody went to school, everybody eventually found their métier. She could empathise with the difficulties faced by others because in many ways she experienced them as her own. She was equally concerned about the fate of strangers, about people living on the street or someone's suitcase being opened by customs officers.

In 1965, she broke her usual silence, endorsing food guru Henry Bieler's book *Food Is Your Best Medicine*. Her friend, the photographer Jean Howard, believed she had given the endorsement out of empathy for people in poor health. Garbo had all but walked in their shoes when, as a young girl, she had nursed her sick father. In the long dark months of New York City's infamous winters, she was often found helping people caught in snow drifts outside her apartment building. She was still pushing cars in her late sixties and seventies. Every Christmas she took eggnog to an elderly couple living on Fifty-seventh Street. On a trip to Reno with Gayelord Hauser in late summer 1939, she complained about the treatment of the calves and bulls at a local rodeo. Soon after she moved into her first Hollywood home at 1027 Chevy Chase Drive, the house began to resemble an animal sanctuary. She adopted a chow, a parrot and two stray cats she named Big Pint and Half Pint.

As a child, Greta earned small change by performing in Stockholm's soup kitchens and gave the coins away to her elderly neighbours to help them buy food. When she worked at PUB department store, she gave all her wages to her mother to help run the family home. She used some of the money she earned from *Gösta Berlings Saga* to have a telephone installed in the family flat. She also bought her mother a ring. Eventually she was able to move her family out of Stockholm to the healthier environment of her farm at Lake Gillen. When the Second World War came, she was forced to move them again. This time she paid for their passage to the United States and helped settle them in Santa Fe, New Mexico.

When John Gilbert's career was in decline, Garbo returned the help he had given her during her first days in Hollywood. Seeing him down on his luck, she fought hard for him to be cast as the male lead in *Queen Christina*. Gilbert recalled how nervous he felt during the making of the film and how considerate, tactful and encouraging she was towards him. In 1930, Gavin Gordon landed a part opposite Garbo in *Romance*. He was overjoyed. Gordon was a former railway clerk from Mississippi who had studied acting in his spare time. This was his first major movie role with the potential to launch his career. Driving to the studio for the first day of shooting, he was involved in a car accident, fracturing his collarbone. He knew that if he was hospitalised, the studio would find another actor to take his place. He made it to the studio but during his first scene, he passed out cold. He woke up in hospital to find Garbo at his bedside. She told him not to worry about losing his part in the film. She stood firm against the studio's repeated attempts to replace him, convincing them to reschedule shooting. The new schedule prioritised those scenes in which his character did not appear, giving him time to recuperate without delaying production.

In early 1926, a fourteen-year-old boy named Joel McCrea was hired as Garbo's double for a horse riding scene in *Torrent*. He was required to ride at speed and pull up abruptly, causing his horse to slide through the mud on its hind legs. After seeing him perform the scene twice, Garbo felt the stunt was too dangerous for a young boy and insisted on doing it herself. Though she played the scene successfully, it was McCrea's performance that was used in the completed film. Her fearlessness prompted McCrea to remark that Garbo was a woman with 'plenty of nerve'.[18] These acts of thoughtfulness belie the misanthropic image of Garbo popularised by the media. After a three month trip to Sweden, Garbo arrived back in New York in March 1929. In the excitement as the great star appeared, a ten-year-old girl, holding up a scrapbook filled with photographs and press clippings, promptly fainted dead away at her feet. Garbo helped revive the child, then asking for a pen, she carefully signed her name in the scrapbook. This was the only time she ever gave an autograph in public.

Having lived through two world wars, Garbo had a strong sense of the cost of conflict, particularly to the young. She told Raymond Daum there must be an end to war so that nobody's sons would be sacrificed again. But in common with Theosophists, she also believed that the human race was not yet sufficiently evolved to achieve this. Garbo's Queen Christina is portrayed as a pacifist who objects vehemently to the unacceptable price of war. She describes the army's flag waving and trumpet playing as nothing more than celebrations for maimed and broken men. Between 1939 and 1945, Garbo turned this ideological position into action, covertly gathering information for the Allies. The British film producer Alexander Korda approached Garbo in December 1939. He was working as an agent for British Intelligence and wanted to know if she would be willing to support the war effort. Her unique position as one of the world's most celebrated women would enable her to gain access to suspected Nazi sympathisers. Her first mission involved the Swedish businessman Axel Wenner-Gren. She had already been introduced to Wenner-Gren by the industrialist Wilhelm Sorensen during her last visit to Sweden so she was well placed to infiltrate his circle. She telephoned Wenner-Gren saying she was bored in New York and missed the sun. This ruse produced an invitation to join him on his yacht in the Bahamas. On 17 February 1940, Garbo chartered a plane to Nassau and boarded the Southern Cross with Wenner-Gren, his wife and their guests, many of whom were believed to be arms and munitions dealers. During a ten-day cruise of the West Indies, Garbo noted the contents of key conversations and reported her findings each time the yacht entered a new port. Her spymaster was Sir William Stephenson of British Security Coordination, best known by his wartime intelligence codename 'Intrepid'. The Southern Cross finally berthed at Miami on 28 February and three days later Garbo flew back to LA.

In the winter of 1942, Garbo considered appearing in an English language remake of the Russian film *The Girl from Leningrad*. Set against the backdrop of the Russia-Finland conflict, the plot follows the fortunes of a young resistance fighter - the girl of the film's title. Garbo withdrew suddenly from the project almost certainly on the advice of her British Intelligence contacts. Playing a resistance fighter on film might have aroused suspicion about her real-life activities and had her war work been discovered by the enemy, it would almost certainly have resulted in her death. After the war, in August 1947, Garbo travelled to London. She had lunch with the Prime Minister, Clement Attlee, then went to the Cabinet War Rooms for a meeting with Winston Churchill. Garbo never revealed the reason for this meeting but it is widely believed to have been a high-level debriefing about her wartime role.

Garbo also made significant donations to charities involved with the war effort. On 12 December 1939, she donated anonymously $5,000 (the equivalent of $100,000 today) to the Finnish Relief Fund to support children orphaned during Stalin's invasion of Finland. Garbo's contract for *The Girl from Leningrad* paid $70,000 immediately with a further $80,000 due on the film's completion. When Garbo dropped out, she returned the first payment to Metro-Goldwyn-Mayer on one condition: she told Louis B. Mayer the money should be donated to the war bonds fund. Garbo also donated large amounts of money to charity during peacetime. In October 1946, she was left a $200,000 fortune (almost $3,500,000 today) by an ardent fan named Edgar H. Donne. Rather than accept the money, Garbo donated it all to charity - the Sister Mary Kenny Polio Foundation.

There was no hint of condescension about Garbo's philanthropy. At no point did she appear to regard herself as helping those who were somehow of lower standing.

Garbo's charity sprang from her unwavering egalitarianism, the feeling of being just the same as anyone else.

Gayelord Hauser once took her to meet King Kennedy, personal assistant to gossip columnist Louella Parsons. Kennedy was gay and involved in a *mariage blanc* to Parsons' lesbian daughter Harriet. Kennedy introduced Garbo to his mother, an elderly grande dame, who referred to Garbo as 'this sweet little girl' and asked her, 'What do you do for a living?' Garbo was delighted. Tallulah Bankhead once remarked that if you treated Garbo like anybody else and gave her no special treatment, she was 'as much fun as the next gal.'[19]

I want to cultivate the art of peace, the art of life.

GARBO IN QUEEN CHRISTINA
METRO-GOLDWYN-MAYER 1933

Self-actualised people's lives have meaning and purpose.

Roberto Assagioli stressed the importance of each individual's search for meaning in life. Herman Hesse wrote in *Demian*, 'Everyone's life is a road to himself, to self-realisation.' In *That Gustafsson Girl*, serialised in *Photoplay* in 1930, the Swedish journalist Åke Sundborg reported Garbo's belief that everyone must find their aim in life and try to achieve it. Garbo believed that a person's life journey should reveal both character and capabilities. She regarded work as the strongest indicator of a life's direction and achievements. For her, work meant the motion picture screen. She strove to evolve as an artist and that endeavour gave her life shape and purpose. At the same time her growing spiritual awareness and self-knowledge supported her creative development. Garbo told the journalist Rilla Page Palmborg that, for her, acting was not simply doing scenes, it was living.

Mercedes de Acosta had a different goal - to find answers to the great questions of existence. In her poem, *Faith*, she wrote:

Today I do not feel that I am groping my way
As I have heretofore done, but a strange exaltation
Is in me as though a star had caught in my hair,
Or as if a piece of the moon had come down and
Brushed against my cheek.

Mercedes once told gossip columnist Elsa Maxwell she looked for elements common to all religions in order to find her own personal truth. She claimed her brain was not confined by geographical or cultural boundaries but was 'universal' in nature. Mercedes thrived on complexity. Garbo's temperament required the polar opposite, simplicity. In *Two-Faced Woman*, Garbo's Katrin stresses the importance of a simple and quiet life to the work of any creative artist. Garbo was attracted to asceticism because of the clarity it could provide. She was not attached to material possessions; her home was spartan and she spent many contented hours alone. When Greta was five years old, her aunt Maria found her sitting by herself lost in a daydream. When asked what she was doing, Greta said she was imagining how one day she would be a great actress. Fifteen years later, she had begun her apprenticeship at PUB department store in Stockholm but still dreamed of becoming an actress. She wrote to her friend Eva Blomgren telling her that, despite her new job selling hats, she had not given up her ambition to act. In the summer of 1922, the director Erik Petschler was shopping at PUB with the actresses Tyra Ryman and Gucken Cederborg. When they reached the millinery department, Greta took the opportunity to ask Ryman, the friendlier of the two women, for Petschler's telephone number. Several days went by before she was able to summon up enough courage to call him and ask for an audition. Petschler was impressed and offered her a part in his film *Luffar-Petter / Peter the Tramp*. After appearing in just two short cinema advertisements for PUB, Greta had gained her first major film role.

Unfortunately, PUB refused to allow her time off to make the film. Greta, however, was supremely confident that her future lay in acting and she took the decision to resign. She left her job, even though shooting would take less than a week and she had no further roles beyond Petschler's film. On her resignation slip she wrote that she was leaving to work in the movies. Within a year she had met Mauritz Stiller, whose own purpose in life, it seemed, was to mould her into the great Greta Garbo. He described to a friend his delight in her progress - she received instruction excellently, followed direction closely and was like wax in his hands. Two years later Garbo and Stiller had set sail for America and Hollywood.

Her first three films for Metro-Goldwyn-Mayer were hugely successful. With a bankable formula on its hands, the studio saw no reason to cast her in any role other than the cold-blooded, vampish women she had played so lucratively. But this was not enough for Garbo. She wanted to extend her creative abilities and to take on more demanding and fulfilling roles. When Metro-Goldwyn-Mayer sent her the script for a film called *Women Love Diamonds*, she said she would play no more 'wicked womens' and refused to attend the costume fittings. A furious Louis B. Mayer suspended her without pay and threatened her with deportation. The result was an impasse that continued for months. Robert Reud, a thirty-year-old theatre producer, offered to marry Garbo to shield her from Mayer's threat. Reud attached no conditions to his proposal, telling her she could file for divorce whenever she liked. He offered his help because he believed she was destined to make important films and, as he wrote to her in a letter dated 31 March 1927, 'The only thing that matters in life is art.' Although she didn't take him up on his offer, she recognised in him someone who shared her belief in the supreme importance of creativity.

John Gilbert admired her strict and uncompromising commitment to the quality of her work. Gilbert told the press that sometimes Garbo would not come to the studio if she felt she could not do herself justice on any given day. This austere perfectionism was undoubtedly the basis of her mastery of the form. Garbo wanted to create art, to play interesting and challenging roles. In 1948, screenwriter Walter Reisch and director Billy Wilder tried to lure her out of retirement. They pitched several ideas to her including *Empress Elizabeth of Austria* and *L'Inconnue de la Seine*. The latter project was inspired by a death mask in the Louvre. Reich and Wilder intended to piece together the life of the unknown woman whose body was fished out of the Seine in mysterious circumstances in the late 1880s. Garbo rejected them all. She told Reisch she wanted to play a clown. The clown would appear male on the surface but underneath 'he' would be a woman. His female fans would write adoring letters and never understand his lack of response. She was most interested in playing characters whose unconventionality gave rise to a perverse tension in the narrative. The writer Robert E. Sherwood recognised Garbo's acute sense of creative purpose. He described her as the greatest actress in the world, comparing her to the legendary Italian performer Eleonora Duse, the soprano Lina Cavalieri and even Helen of Troy. According to Kenneth Tynan, watching Garbo on screen was to become enraptured by beauty without vanity. The critic Richard Whitehall described her as a creative artist in the strongest sense who had made cinema-going a richer experience. Even Bette Davis felt moved to praise Garbo, describing her acting as sheer witchcraft. Nobody, she said, could work such mastery.

Garbo believed in the freedom of the individual and equality between the sexes. Many of her characters reflect these feminist ideals. Anna Christie expounds her views as an independent woman, saying she will not be dictated to by men. Karin Borg tells her husband that marriage is an equal partnership. Again and again, Garbo's films promoted ideas considered radical for the time. As early as 1929, feminism was a major theme in *The Single Standard*. The film opens with the caption: 'For a number of generations men have done as they pleased and women have done as men pleased.' Garbo's character, Arden Stuart, leads the progressive challenge as she searches for a single standard of conduct that can apply to both sexes. She finds an ally in Packy Cannon (Nils Asther) who tells her that love between men and women should always be founded on equality and perfect freedom. This groundbreaking film shows Garbo beginning to pull the rug, albeit it gently, from underneath the patriarchy. In *Queen Christina* Garbo advocates peace for her country. She wants to develop a new international model for the world, one that is founded on egalitarianism and happiness. She tells her obstinate Lord Chancellor that people have blindly followed generals to their own destruction but now she can lead them in a new direction to beauty, gaiety and freedom.

Like anyone on the path to self-actualisation, Garbo was driven to find meaning and purpose in her life. Initially, she found that purpose in acting, then later in her exploration of the occult. Throughout, she stayed true to her progressive, egalitarian principles. She was a committed non-conformist, the outsider who, as Colin Wilson put it, seeks a course of action where she can be most herself and in which she 'achieves the maximum self-expression'.[20] Perhaps it was this emphatic self-realisation that prompted the film critic Hollis Alpert to wonder if she were something other than an actor, if she were perhaps a phenomenon beyond acting, a phenomenon of nature.

I am afraid of nothing, except being bored.

GARBO IN CAMILLE
METRO-GOLDWYN-MAYER 1936

Self-actualised people live their lives free from fear.

Laila Gumpel was the daughter of the swimmer Max Gumpel. When Garbo stayed with the Gumpels at their family home, just outside Stockholm, she would often spend hours playing with Laila and her sister Margareta. During one of her stays, Garbo asked Laila to vow that she would never let money, fame or other people control her life. These words reveal the true nature of Garbo's modus vivendi. She was unaltered by money or fame. She was impervious to public opinion. She travelled her own path without fear, much to the exasperation of men like Howard Dietz. As Metro-Goldwyn-Mayer's Head of Publicity, Dietz was one of the most influential figures in Hollywood, used to bending actors effortlessly to his will. Garbo alone would not yield. She criticised Hollywood openly during interviews and Dietz was unable to intimidate her into silence however hard he tried. Louis B. Mayer wielded even greater power than Dietz but this simply made no difference to Garbo. In the spring of 1926, Mauritz Stiller was appointed to direct Garbo's second film, *The Temptress*. Shooting began on 17 April but the production was fraught with problems from the outset. Stiller declined to have an interpreter on set and his instructions to actors and camera operators were often misunderstood. Added to this, he refused to follow the standard practice of shooting scenes in sequence, something which antagonised both Mayer and producer Irving Thalberg. When news of Stiller's affair with his male secretary, Carlo Keil-Moller, reached Mayer, the Metro-Goldwyn-Mayer boss wasted no time in dismissing Stiller once and for all. On 27 April, Garbo was summoned to Irving Thalberg's office and told the news that Stiller had been fired. She listened in silence then asked for her car to be brought back onto the Metro-Goldwyn-Mayer lot. She turned her back on Thalberg and left, driving out to a small hotel in Santa Monica and refusing to reveal her whereabouts to anyone. When she eventually surfaced, she told Mayer she would return to work but she also threatened to sue him for sacking Stiller. In her absence, the Danish costume designer Max Rée had become another casualty, resigning because Thalberg had ordered the destruction of every one of the costumes designed during Stiller's tenure. Garbo was not prepared to stand by as members of the crew were bullied or treated unjustly. She stood up to Thalberg's heavy-handed tactics and walked out on the production for a second time. Stiller's replacement, Fred Niblo, came up with a workable compromise. He would rehire Rée and compensate the designer for his lost income out of his own pocket. Garbo was satisfied and returned to work. By the time shooting wrapped on 26 July, Garbo had developed a firm friendship with Niblo and gave him a signed picture with the words: 'To Fred Niblo, with a piece of my heart.' Less than two months later Mayer and Garbo locked horns again. On 18 September 1926, Garbo's agent pushed Mayer for a pay rise. Garbo was Metro-Goldwyn-Mayer's biggest asset and as a matter of principle she deserved to be paid the same as any male lead. Mayer would not budge. Again, Garbo refused to attend the studio, this time retreating to

La Quinta, a resort just outside of Palm Springs. As pre-production on her next film, *Love*, ground to a halt, Mayer realised his hard-line attitude was getting him nowhere. The mighty studio head was forced to give in. On 1 June 1927, Garbo signed a new contract with equal pay which was also backdated for the five months she had declined to work.

Whenever Garbo was on the studio floor, she insisted on a closed set. Acting was her focus and she insisted on giving it her full concentration without distractions. Ardent male admirers often asked if they could watch her work. Garbo always said no regardless of how important the man behind the request might be. During the making of *Romance*, the studio attempted to disguise the presence of the powerful *Los Angeles Times* film critic, Phil Scheuer, by hiding him in darkness at the back of the sound stage. Sensing something was amiss, Garbo peered into the distance beyond the mass of extras. She fixed her eyes on Scheuer's hiding place and demanded he be escorted from the premises before she would consent to continue with the shoot.

Between 1924 and 1929, John Gilbert was the most successful and sought after male lead in Hollywood. Gilbert and Garbo's first kiss in the 1926 film *Flesh and the Devil* marked the beginning of their turbulent romance. Any relationship between two such mercurial artists was bound to be volatile. Every time they clashed, Gilbert was determined not to give in. He would instruct his housekeeper to say he was out if Miss Garbo phoned. Every hour he would ask, has Miss Garbo called? The answer would always be no. By the end of the day, he would tell his housekeeper to get Miss Garbo on the phone! Garbo's indomitable attitude to powerful men is reflected in a number of her roles. As Elena in *The Temptress*, she confronts the ruthless bandit, Manos Duras. She tells him that even though he strikes terror in other men's hearts, she is not afraid of him. In *Mata Hari*, her identity as a spy is revealed by a jealous lover. Her spymaster, Andriani, orders her to flee France to save herself. She tells him, 'What do I care for your orders? You can't frighten me.'

Garbo became known for the phrase, 'I think I go home now.' This was what she told Louis B. Mayer every time they came to yet another impasse over contracts, scripts or co-stars. The actor Colleen Moore, a close friend of John Gilbert, described Mayer's predicament perfectly: 'You can't really argue with someone who is just as happy to go home if she doesn't get her way.'[21]

Garbo approached a multitude of challenges without fear. In October 1927, one of the greatest challenges of her career appeared on the horizon with the premiere of the first talking picture. *The Jazz Singer*, starring Al Jolson, became an overnight sensation. It sounded the death knell of the silent movie. The public and a scandal-hungry press eagerly awaited each major star's first appearance in a talking picture. Art Acord was Hollywood's first cowboy heartthrob, an image carefully constructed by the studio around his rugged looks and his background as a rodeo champion. In silent Westerns, he portrayed characters with names like 'Hairtrigger Jordan' and 'Two-gun O'Brien'. His career ended abruptly with the advent of talking pictures because his voice was too light to sustain his image as a macho gunslinger. THE MICROPHONE - THE TERROR OF THE STUDIOS declared the cover of *Photoplay* in December 1929 beside a picture of silent film star Norma Talmadge. Prophetically the tagline read YOU CAN'T GET AWAY WITH IT IN HOLLYWOOD. Talmadge had a thick Brooklyn accent which was at odds with her image as the refined and glamorous star of silent film. Even though she hired a voice coach in preparation for her first talking picture, her career could not be saved. A review in *Time* magazine, published 17 November 1930, criticised Talmadge for talking like an elocution pupil in her first sound role (*New York Nights*, United Artists, 1929) and like an elocution teacher in her second (*Du Barry - A Woman of Passion*, United Artists, 1930).

The greatest humiliation was the one waiting for John Gilbert who made his talking picture debut in Metro-Goldwyn-Mayer's 1929 film, *His Glorious Night*. Louis B. Mayer couldn't wait to be rid of the outspoken actor and set out to engineer his downfall. Early in their relationship, Gilbert had deeply offended the moralistic Mayer when he jokingly described his mother, Ida Gilbert, as a whore. Mayer was extremely close to his own mother and was furious at what he considered to be Gilbert's attack on the sanctity of motherhood. From then on Mayer and Gilbert bickered constantly. The tension between the two men only increased as Gilbert made repeated efforts to marry Garbo. Such a union would have made them Hollywood's most powerful couple, a prospect Mayer did not relish. On 8 September 1926, Gilbert attempted to get Garbo to the altar once more. He suggested a double wedding with his friends, the director King Vidor and the actor Eleanor Boardman. Once again he was thwarted when Garbo vanished on the morning of Vidor and Boardman's nuptials. Unable to stop himself, Mayer baited Gilbert viciously. Slapping him on the back, Mayer asked him why he needed to marry Garbo anyway. He suggested Gilbert should simply screw her, then forget about it. Gilbert was incensed. He shoved Mayer to the ground, causing him to hit his head and break his glasses. Livid with rage, Mayer rounded on Gilbert, telling him he would destroy him even if it cost him a million dollars. His chance finally came with the advent of sound. During the filming of *His Glorious Night*, the sound technician was instructed to turn the bass down and the treble up whenever Gilbert spoke. This gave Gilbert's voice an uncannily high-pitched timbre. When the film premiered and Gilbert shrilly uttered the words 'I love you, I love you, I love you' to Catherine Dale Owen, audiences fell about laughing. Gilbert's position as Hollywood's Great Lover was effectively destroyed. His career in sudden ruins, he became an alcoholic. On 9 January 1936, he suffered a heart attack and was found dead at his home in Beverley Hills. He was just thirty-six years old. Gilbert's ex-wife, Leatrice Joy, saw *His*

Glorious Night in Milwaukee where she was appearing in a variety show. She believed Gilbert's pairing with Dale Owen contributed to the film's failure: 'All that kissing and saying "I love you" looked all the more ridiculous with her because she was such a cold fish. The audience laughed and so did I. I couldn't help it.'[22] According to Louis B. Mayer's daughter Irene, when the first reviews came in, Mayer took them home, threw them on the dining table and said, 'That should take care of Mr. Gilbert.'[23] Nine days after the opening of *His Glorious Night, Anna Christie* went into production. Garbo was next in the firing line.

Garbo showed no fear at the prospect of her first foray into talking pictures. She calmly announced that if the studio wanted her to speak in a film, then she would speak in a film. Shooting wrapped on 18 November 1929 and the Metro-Goldwyn-Mayer publicity machine went into full swing. All across America billboards declared: 'Garbo Talks!' As the premiere approached, studio executives became increasingly nervous. They were unable to scupper reports of impending doom. Rumours abounded that Garbo was readying herself for disaster, closing up her house and preparing to leave for Sweden. *Anna Christie* premiered in Hollywood on 22 January 1930. When Garbo appeared, almost twenty minutes into the film, moviegoing audiences held their breath. In her first scene, she enters a bar, sits down and says to the barman in husky tones, 'Gimme a viskey, ginger ale on the side, and don't be stingy baby!' From that moment the public was smitten, enchanted by her richly accented baritone voice. *Picture Play*'s influential film critic, Norbert Lusk, called it the voice that shook the world. Richard Watts of the *Herald Tribune* described its poetic glamour. Mordaunt Hall of *The New York Times* admired the way her deep tones seemed to compel the viewer's attention. Garbo made the transition smoothly from silent movies to talkies because she was not afraid of failure. If her career had been destroyed by her speaking voice, she would simply have taken a different path in life. She refused to be a hostage to fortune. Neither success nor failure held any power over her. In the early days of sound, every studio had a projector on set. The technician would run the projector forwards and backwards so the director could check continuity. Garbo delighted in watching talking pictures played in reverse. She roared with laughter at the peculiar sound of her lines spoken backwards. She laughed in the face of the talkies and as a consequence they could not harm her.

In *Mata Hari*, General Shubin (Lionel Barrymore) tells Garbo to hurry back to her lodgings as they are in imminent danger of being searched by the police. She says she has no intention of rushing away on account of something she refuses to believe will happen. Garbo lived her own life undaunted by what *might* happen. On their arrival in America, Garbo and Stiller languished in New York's Hotel Commodore throughout the sweltering summer months. Studio executives declined to speak with Stiller and he became increasingly disconsolate. Garbo, on the other hand, possessed a steely determination. During the long, stiflingly hot days, she refused to give in to misery and remained focused on her purpose to become an actor in Hollywood. One of Stiller's acquaintances in New York was the Swedish actor Martha Hedman. She introduced Garbo and Stiller to celebrity photographer Arnold Genthe. (Genthe had photographed numerous stars including the stage actors Eva La Galliene and Diana Barrymore.) Garbo suggested she would like to be photographed by Genthe some day. It was as if she were guided by the same force described by the writer Lyall Watson as 'that still, small voice that whispers "No" when we make a bad move, or simply says "Stop, that's it," when we hit upon the right solution.'[24] Genthe insisted he photograph her that afternoon. Genthe's portraits caught Garbo's mystical and ethereal presence perfectly. When studio executives saw Genthe's pictures they performed a sudden volte-face, telling Stiller that he and Garbo were to board the next train to Los Angeles. Within a few weeks she was cast as Leonora Moreno in *Torrent*, the first of a string of Garbo box office hits.

Garbo was drawn to women who radiated confidence and resolve. She enjoyed Salka Viertel's company because Viertel was artistic but also determined. One friend described Viertel as predatory in the way she pursued life. Garbo was attracted to Mercedes de Acosta for similar reasons. It was Mercedes who had originally held a vision of Garbo in her mind, telling her Paris friends in 1929 that she was going to Hollywood 'to meet Greta Garbo'. But Garbo was interested in these two women for another reason. They were not afraid to be different. Both stood out as misfits in Hollywood, as genuine outsiders against a backdrop of hollow celebrity culture. Viertel was the archetypal European exile in America. She hosted a regular salon attended by creative people such as F.W. Murnau, William Dieterle, Tallulah Bankhead and, of course, Garbo. Mercedes, meanwhile, cut a striking figure as the trousered Sapphic poet. The free-spirited vitality of both women was refreshing to Garbo who lived her own life in fearless non-conformity. As a Hollywood film star, she defied type. Louella Parsons and Hedda Hopper were the two most powerful gossip columnists in America. Garbo was the first actor to refuse both of them an interview. She never looked at her fan mail. She declined to give autographs. Her strength of character and her courage in saying 'no' made her all the more precious to her fans. *Photoplay*'s Leonard Hall observed that Garbo could get away with the kind of eccentricity that would send other movie stars' fans 'shrieking away in droves'. Gilbert Adrian, Garbo's costume designer for most of her Hollywood career, said she so consistently lived life her own way that, regardless of her critics, she could not help but be different.

Ultimately, Garbo's most fearless act was to turn her back on the movies and walk away. She told Sven Broman that she simply became tired of Hollywood. She became tired of the media's relentless pursuit. Garbo chose to put her self above her image. To continue to be part of the film industry came at too high a price. After the release of *Two-*

Faced Woman, Mercedes claimed Garbo told her she would never act in another film. In the years that followed, Garbo was offered a plethora of parts. She would not return to the screen unless she could play distinctly unorthodox roles. Her demands for originality were too much for Hollywood. Those roles never materialised and she never compromised in this regard.

She was an authentic spiritual explorer, an independent thinker who had no need of the approbation of others. In common with all self-actualised people, she was unafraid of solitude, using times of quiet contemplation to consider profound metaphysical questions. Perhaps John Gilbert summed up the mystery of Garbo best: 'One day, she is childlike, naive, ingenious, a girl of ten. The next day she is a mysterious woman a thousand years old, knowing everything, baffling, deep. Garbo has more sides to her personality than anyone I have ever met.'

END

Advertisements

1920

Mr and Mrs Stockholm Go Shopping /
Herrskapet Stockholm Ute På Inköp

An advertisement for PUB department store.
Garbo appears in the sequence called How Not to Dress.

1921
Our Daily Bread
An advertisement for the Stockholm Co-operative Society's Bakery Department.

Silent films
1922
Peter the Tramp / Luffar-Petter (released 26 December)
Directed by Erik Petschler
Garbo plays Greta Nordberg

An army officer falls in love with the Mayor's daughter, Greta Nordberg.
While he takes her bathing, a tramp steals his uniform and impersonates him.

1924
Gösta Berlings Saga (Two Parts)
(Part One released 10 March, Part Two released 17 March)
Directed by Mauritz Stiller
Garbo plays Countess Elizabeth Dohna

Gösta Berling is a priest who has been expelled from the church. He becomes a
tutor for a noble family and meets Countess Elizabeth Dohna. After a string of
affairs, the disgraced priest realises it is Elizabeth he truly loves and they begin
a new life together.

1925
The Joyless Street / Die Freudlose Gasse (released 18 May)
Directed by G. W. Pabst
Garbo plays Grete Rumfort

Set in and around a street called Melchiorgasse in post-war Austria, the story
centres on two young women from the same deprived neighbourhood. While her
friend Maria becomes a prostitute, Grete is rescued from the same fate by her
relationship with an American Red Cross officer.

1926
Torrent (released 21 February)
Directed by Monta Bell
Garbo plays Leonora Moreno

Leonora and Don Rafael are star-crossed lovers. His mother disapproves of her impoverished family and Leonora leaves to pursue a singing career in Paris. Even though she later returns a success, Rafael's mother still rejects her. Rafael marries another woman but years later seeks out Leonora, telling her he still loves her. Leonora cannot allow him to leave his wife and children. She turns him down, deciding to continue with her singing career.

1926
The Temptress (released 10 October)
Directed by Fred Niblo
Garbo plays Elena

Elena is a vamp who unwittingly destroys the lives of the men she becomes involved with. Her husband prostitutes her to wealthy benefactors but she meets and falls for Robledo, an engineer. When Robledo discovers her lifestyle he is disgusted and rejects her, leaving for Argentina to work on the construction of a dam. She follows him but brings disaster to the local village when a bandit falls for her and Robledo is forced to fight a duel with him. The bandit blows up the dam, flooding the village and Robledo sends Elena away for good. She falls into ruin and becomes a penniless prostitute in Paris.

1927
Flesh and the Devil (released 9 January)
Directed by Clarence Brown
Garbo plays Felicitas

Leo and Ulrich are soldiers and childhood friends. Leo falls in love with Felicitas, the wife of a count. He kills the count in a duel and is sent away from the military in disgrace. On his return he finds Felicitas has married Ulrich. Felicitas and Leo rekindle their passion but are discovered by Ulrich. The two friends duel and, as she rushes across a frozen lake to stop them, Felicitas falls through the ice and drowns.

1927
Love (released 29 November)
Directed by Edmund Goulding
Garbo plays Anna Karenina

An adaptation of Tolstoy's novel Anna Karenina. Anna is the wife of a Russian senator. She falls for Count Alexei Vronsky, an army officer, and leaves her husband to become his mistress. Vronsky's reputation and army career suffer as a result and, to save him further disgrace, she commits suicide, throwing herself under a train.

1928
The Divine Woman (released 14 January)
Directed by Victor Seastrom
Garbo plays Marianne

Marianne is a young actress who must choose between two men, Lucien, an impoverished soldier who goes to jail for stealing a dress for her and Legrande, a wealthy Parisian theatre producer. Ultimately she chooses Lucien and the pair marry, running away to South America. The plot is based on the early life of actress Sarah Bernhardt.

1928
The Mysterious Lady (released 4 August)
Directed by Fred Niblo
Garbo plays Tania Fedorova

Captain Karl von Raden is an Austrian army officer who falls in love with Tania, a Russian spy. She steals the secret documents he was to deliver to Berlin and he is court-martialled. Released from prison, he goes to Russia to find her. She convinces him of the truth that she really loves him and he helps her escape back to Austria so they can be together.

1929

A Woman of Affairs (released 19 January)
Directed by Clarence Brown
Garbo plays Diana Merrick

*Diana is in love with Neville Montague but his father opposes the relationship.
Neville is sent away and Diana marries another man, who later commits
suicide when he is revealed to be an embezzler. When she is reunited with
Neville, he is married, but they spend the night together. Realising her return
may ruin Neville's reputation, she leaves. As she drives away in distress, she
crashes her car into a tree and is killed.*

1929

Wild Orchids (released 30 March)
Directed by Sidney Franklin
Garbo plays Lillie Sterling

*Lillie Sterling and her husband John are travelling to Java where he plans to
invest in a tea plantation. They become friends with a Javanese prince with
whom Lillie later has an affair. Discovering her infidelity, John plans to leave
but Lillie is waiting for him in his car and declares her love for him.*

1929

A Man's Man (released 25 May)
Directed by James Cruz

*Garbo, John Gilbert and director Fred Niblo make cameo appearances in
documentary footage. The film is based on Patrick Kearney's Broadway play,
A Man's Man.*

1929

The Single Standard (released 27 July)
Directed by John S. Robertson
Garbo plays Arden Stuart

*Arden falls in love with Packy Cannon, a wealthy painter, but their romance
cannot compete with his desire to paint. She marries her long-term admirer,
Tommy Hewlett. When Packy returns to her, she contemplates running away
with him, but eventually chooses her marriage over him and decides to remain
with her husband and child.*

1929
The Kiss (released 15 November)
Directed by Jacques Feyder
Garbo plays Irene Guarry

Irene's jealous husband pulls out a gun when he catches a young admirer forcing himself on her. In the ensuing mayhem, she wrestles the gun away and accidentally kills her husband. During her trial she is defended by a lawyer who is a former lover. He eventually gains her acquittal.

Talking pictures

1930
Anna Christie (released 4 March)
Directed by Clarence Brown
Garbo plays Anna Christie

Anna comes to live with her impecunious father on his barge in New York. She meets a rowdy young sailor who falls in love with her. Feeling conflicted, she is compelled to tell him of her past life as a prostitute and he leaves her. However, he later comes to realise how much he loves her and returns.

A German language version was also filmed and released on 2 December.

1930
Romance (released 22 August)
Directed by Clarence Brown
Garbo plays Rita Cavallini

Rita is an opera singer who is the mistress of the wealthy Cornelius van Tuyl. She meets a young rector called Tom Armstrong and they fall in love. Rita realises that ultimately they cannot be together as the relationship would ruin his reputation and she sends him away.

1931
Inspiration (released 6 February)
Directed by Clarence Brown
Garbo plays Yvonne Valbret

Andre Montell, a young diplomat, falls in love with Yvonne Valbret, an artist's model. Her past includes many former lovers and, even though he wants to marry her, she decides to leave him to save his good name.

1931
Susan Lenox: Her Fall and Rise (released 16 October)
Directed by Robert Z. Leonard
Garbo plays Susan Lenox

Running away from an arranged marriage, Susan begins a relationship with Rodney Spencer. Her father catches up with her and she escapes again, this time joining the circus. The leader of the circus, Wayne Burlingham, forces himself on her. When Rodney finds her there, he mistakenly believes the two are together and rejects her. Susan follows Rodney to South America where they reunite and begin a new life.

1931
Mata Hari (released 31 December)
Directed by George Fitzmaurice
Garbo plays Mata Hari

The film traces the romance between the German spy Mata Hari and a Russian pilot with whom she falls in love. He is later injured in a plane crash. When Mata Hari's identity as a spy is revealed, rather than flee, she chooses to remain with her injured lover. She is captured and sentenced to death by firing squad.

1932
Grand Hotel (released 12 April)
Directed by Edmund Goulding
Garbo plays Grusinskaya

Grusinskaya is a lonely ballet dancer who falls in love with a jewel thief. Shortly before she plans to leave with him to begin a new life, he is killed during an attempted burglary.

1932
As You Desire Me (released 2 June)
Directed by George Fitzmaurice
Garbo plays Zara/Maria

The film is based on the play by Luigi Pirandello. Zara is a cabaret singer in Budapest. Suffering from amnesia, she lives with novelist Carl Salter. It is discovered that she may be Maria Varelli, the long lost wife of an Italian count. Zara goes to live with the count and tries to regain her memory. Salter tries to get her back, producing a woman he claims is the count's long-lost wife. She is proven to be an impostor and Zara remains with Count Varelli.

1933

Queen Christina (released 26 December)
Directed by Rouben Mamoulian
Garbo plays Queen Christina

The film is based on the life of the 17th-century Swedish monarch. Queen Christina falls in love with the Spanish ambassador, Don Antonio. She abdicates but before she can run away with him, he is killed in a duel by the jealous and scheming Count Magnus. She leaves Sweden to face exile alone.

1934

The Painted Veil (released 7 December)
Directed by Richard Boleslawski
Garbo plays Katrin Fane

Katrin's husband, Walter, is a doctor posted to China. He neglects her and she has an affair with the British attaché, Jack Townsend. When her husband discovers the affair, he forces her to go to the hinterland with him to fight a cholera epidemic. Despite their problems, Katrin and Walter gradually begin to fall in love again.

1935

Anna Karenina (released 30 August)
Directed by Clarence Brown
Garbo plays Anna Karenina

The film is a reworking of the original silent movie, Love, based on Tolstoy's novel.

1937

Camille (released 22 January)
Directed by George Cukor
Garbo plays Camille

Camille is a Parisian courtesan who falls in love with a young man, Armand Duval. His father intercedes and Camille ends the relationship to save Armand's reputation and career. Eventually she contracts tuberculosis and, when Armand returns to be with her again, she dies in his arms.

1937
Marie Walewska / aka Conquest (released 4 November)
Directed by Clarence Brown
Garbo plays Marie Walewska

Marie is a Polish countess who becomes Napoleon's mistress. Napoleon is later forced to marry a Hapsburg princess to consolidate his power. Marie is forced to leave, keeping it secret that she is pregnant with his child. Years later, on the final night before Napoleon's exile, Marie returns to him to show him the son she secretly gave birth to after their affair ended.

1939
Ninotchka (released 9 November)
Directed by Ernst Lubitsch
Garbo plays Ninotchka

Ninotchka is sent to Paris to supervise three bumbling Soviet envoys who are trying to sell jewels confiscated by the Communist government. She meets and falls in love with the suave Count Leon d'Algout. She abandons Communism and Russia to be with him.

1941
Two-Faced Woman (released 31 December)
Directed by George Cukor
Garbo plays Karin Borg and Kathryn Borg

Ski instructor Karin is swept off her feet by magazine editor Larry Blake. They hastily marry but Larry expects her to be dutiful and move to New York with him. She refuses. On Larry's return to New York, his old flame Griselda seduces him. Karin decides to pose as her fictitious and carefree twin sister in order to entice and ultimately win back her errant husband from Griselda's clutches. Karin succeeds and she and Larry are reunited.

1. *Robert Payne, The Great Garbo, W.H. Allen, 1976.*

2. *Ibid.*

3. *Abraham Maslow, Toward A Psychology of Being, Van Nostrand, 1968.*

4. *Roberto Assagioli, Psychosynthesis, Hobbs Dorman, 1965.*

5. *Kevin Brownlow interview of Ricardo Cortez, 28 October 1965.*

6. *Assagioli, ibid.*

7. *Mercedes de Acosta, Here Lies the Heart, Reynal Press, 1960.*

8. *Hollis Alpert, The Saga of Greta Lovisa Gustafsson, The New York Times, September 1965.*

9. *Nathaniel Benchley, This Is Garbo, Collier's magazine, 1 March, 1952.*

10. *Rilla Page Palmborg, The Private Life of Greta Garbo, Doubleday, 1931.*

11. *de Acosta, ibid.*

12. *Ibid.*

13. *Ibid.*

14. *Raymond Daum, Walking With Garbo, Harper Collins, 1991.*

15. *Gary Lachman, The Quest For Hermes Trismegistus, Floris Books, 2011.*

16. *Assagioli, ibid.*

17. *Daum, ibid.*

18. *Barry Paris, Garbo, Alfred A. Knopf, 1994 (quoting The Brooklyn Eagle 1 March 1942).*

19. *Daum, ibid.*

20. *Colin Wilson, The Outsider, Victor Gollancz, 1956.*

21. *Leatrice Gilbert Fountain, Dark Star - The Meteoric Rise and Eclipse of John Gilbert, Sidgwick and Jackson, 1985.*

22. *Ibid.*

23. *Ibid.*

24. *Lyall Watson, Beyond Supernature, Bantam Books, 1987.*

Acosta, Mercedes de, Here Lies the Heart, Reynal Press, 1960.

Assagioli, Roberto, Psychosynthesis, Hobbs Dorman, 1965.

Blavatsky, Helena Petrovna, The Key to Theosophy, Theosophical University Press 1889.

Brett, David, Greta Garbo Divine Star, The Robson Press, 2012.

Broman, Sven, Conversations With Garbo, Viking Penguin, 1992.

Charles River Editors, Legends of Hollywood The Life And Legacy of Greta Garbo, 2013.

Daum, Raymond, Walking With Garbo, Harper Collins, 1991.

Fountain, Leatrice Gilbert, Dark Star - The Meteoric Rise and Eclipse of John Gilbert, Sidgwick and Jackson, 1985.

Hauser, Gaylord, Eat and Grow Beautiful, Faber and Faber, 1948.

Jinarajadasa, C., Practical Theosophy, Theosophical Publishing House, 1918.

Lachman, Gary, The Quest For Hermes Trismegistus, Floris Books, 2011.

Lachman, Gary, Beyond the Robot: The Life and Work of Colin Wilson, Tarcher Perigee, 2016.

Leadbeater, C.W., A Textbook of Theosophy, Freeriver, 1912.

Maslow, Abraham, Toward a Psychology of Being, Van Nostrand, 1968.

Paris, Barry, Garbo, Alfred A. Knopf, 1994.

Payne, Robert, The Great Garbo, W.H. Allen, 1976.

Souhami, Diana, Greta and Cecil, Random House, 1994.

Vickers, Hugo, Loving Garbo, Jonathan Cape,1994.

Watson, Lyall, Beyond Supernature, Bantam Books, 1987.

Wilber, Ken, Integral Meditation, Shambhala, 2016.

Wilson, Colin, The Outsider, Victor Gollancz, 1956.

Wilson, Colin, New Pathways In Psychology, Taplinger, 1972.

Wilson, Colin, Super Consciousness, Watkins, 2009.

Wyatt, Tim, Cycles of Eternity, Firewheel, 2016.

Zierold, Norman, Garbo, W.H. Allen, 1970.

Alpert, Hollis, The Saga of Greta Lovisa Gustafsson, The New York Times, September 1965.

Benchley, Nathaniel, This Is Garbo, Collier's magazine, 1 March 1952.

Brownlow, Kevin, Ricardo Cortez interview, 28 October 1965.

Palmborg, Rilla Page, The Private Life of Greta Garbo, Doubleday, 1931.

A

Acord, Art 166
Acosta, Mercedes de 43, 57, 76, 83, 86-87, 94-95, 97, 100, 108, 111, 117, 119-20, 123-31, 133, 136-37, 139, 141, 155-56, 171-73
Adolphson, Edvin 80
Adrian 83, 127, 172
All Quiet on the Western Front 38
Alpert, Hollis 160
Anna Christie 23, 74, 77, 101, 124, 169
Anna Karenina 20-21, 86, 138
As You Desire Me 85
Assagioli, Roberto 32, 55, 59, 115, 139, 155
Asther, Nils 57, 94, 112, 159
Attlee, Clement 88-89, 151
Ayres, Lew 37-38, 76

B

Baba, Sri Meher 123, 127-28
Baer, Max 45-46
Baker, Josephine 140
Balzac, Honoré de 58
Bankhead, Tallulah 136, 152, 172
Bardelys the Magnificent 65
Barrymore, Diana 171
Barrymore, Georgina Drew 78
Barrymore, John 44, 78
Barrymore, Lionel 78, 170
Beaton, Cecil 20, 32, 48, 59, 69, 73-75, 78, 88, 95, 110, 117, 123, 126, 129, 133, 138-39

Behrman, S.N. 145
Ben Hur 53
Bennet, Constance 26
Bernadotte, Carl Johan 49, 116
Bernadotte, Kerstin 49, 116
Bickford, Charles 24, 101
Bieler, Henry 146
Billings, Lem 103
Blavatsky, Helena 31, 125, 129
Blomgren, Eva 156
Boardman, Eleanor 168
Bohr, Nils 47-48
Borg, Sven Hugo 33-34, 43, 64, 75, 100
Brecht, Berthold 65
Breen, Joseph 99
Broman, Sven 22, 116, 129, 172
Bromfield, Louis 19
Brooks, Louise 100
Brown, Clarence 21, 68-69, 133
Brown, Johnny Mack 23, 101
Brownlow, Kevin 54
Brunton, Paul 127

C

Camille 46, 109, 124, 129
Carl XVI Gustav, king of Sweden 79
Cavalieri, Lina 159
Cederborg, Gucken 156
Christie, Agatha 83
Christina, Queen 21, 31, 98
Christopher Bean 77
Churchill , Winston 83, 89, 151
Claire, Ina 36-37, 96

Cocteau, Jean 140
Collm, Maria 100
Cooley, Eleanor S. 130
Cooper, Lady Diana 138
Cornell, Joseph 68
Cortez, Ricardo 24, 54
Crawford, Joan 57, 77-78, 93
Cukor, George 46, 73

D
Daniels, William 20, 145
Danielson, Emilie 64
Daudet, Alphonse 69
Daum, Raymond 3, 93-95, 141, 145, 149
Davies, Marion 64
Davis, Bette 159
Diamond, David 37, 110
Dieterle, William 172
Dietrich, Marlene 47
Dietz, Howard 23, 54, 109-10, 163
Dinner at Eight 77
Donne, Edgar H. 151
Douglas, Melvyn 24, 36, 102, 112
Dr. Jekyll and Mr. Hyde 43
Dressler, Marie 76-77
Drimmer, Eric 89
Du Barry - A Woman of Passion 167
Duchesse de Langeais, La 58
Duff, Michael 78
Dumas, Alexandre 46
Duncan, Isadora 129-30
Durlacher Brothers 110
Duse, Eleonora 159

E
Engberg, John 78
Erickson, Leif 123

F
Fairbanks, Douglas 103
Fairbanks Jnr, Douglas 101
Fawcett, George 101
Feyder, Jacques 76
Flesh And The Devil 69, 96, 101, 165
Franklin, Sidney 145

G
Gable, Clarke 44, 96
Galliene, Eva la 171
Gandhi 83, 133
Genthe, Arnold 171
Gert, Valeska 100
Gibran, Kahlil 123
Gilbert, Ida 167
Gilbert, John 21, 23, 33, 36, 43, 45, 56, 65-66, 69, 79, 84, 96-7, 100-101, 135, 148, 158, 165-69, 173
Girl from Leningrad, The 150-51
Goldstein, Kurt 13
Gone With the Wind 26
Gordon, Gavin 107, 148
Goulding, Edmund 20
Gösta Berlings Saga 13, 53, 65, 83, 134, 147
Grand Hotel 77-78
Grant, Joan 134
Green, Sam 34, 47, 49, 50, 69, 88, 96, 126, 134, 138
Gunther, Jane Perry 59, 109

Gumpel, Laila 163
Gumpel, Margareta 163
Gumpel, Max 43, 78
Gustaf V, king of Sweden 48
Gustafsson, Alva Maria 11
Gustafsson, Greta Lovisa 11,
19, 89
Gustafsson, Karl Alfred 11
Gustafsson (Garbo), Sven 79

H
Hale, Alan 101
Hall, Leonard 172
Hall, Mordaunt 59, 170
Hamilton, Sara 78
Hanson, Einar 35-36, 140,
145-46
Hanson, Lars 64, 101
Harlow, Jean 83
Hauser, Gayelord 88, 94, 132,
147, 152
Hays Code 98-99
Hays, Will 98,
Hedman, Martha 171
Hepburn, Katherine 33
Her Big Night 146
Herbert, David 78
Here Lies the Heart 86-87, 133
Herzog, Dorothy 20
Hesse, Herman 155
His Glorious Night 167-69
Hitler, Adolf 45-47, 100
Hopper, Hedda 172
How Not to Dress 55
Howard, Jean 147
Huxley, Aldous 130-31

I
Inspiration 24, 68, 110, 119
Ibsen, Henrik 65
Isherwood, Christopher 131

J
Jazz Singer, The 166
Jinarajadasa, C. 130
Jolson, Al 166
Joy, Leatrice 168
Judge, William Quan 125
Jupp, Kenneth 25, 107

K
Karlsson, Anna Lovisa 11
Keil-Moller, Carlo 163
Kennedy, Jackie 103
Kennedy, King 152
Kirk, Poppy 137
Kiss, The 37, 76, 94
Korda, Alexander 149
Krishnamurti, Jiddu 130-31

L
Lachman, Gary 135
Lagerlöf, Selma 53
Leigh Vivien 26-27
Leonard, Robert Z. 44
Lewis, Sinclair 133
Loos, Anita 125
Love 20, 165
Lubitsch, Ernst 22, 26, 56
Lusk, Norbert 170

M
Magnusson, Charles 13
Maharshi, Ramana 123, 127-28

Mailer, Norman 26
Malcolm, Elizabeth 118
Malina, Judith 107
Mann, Thomas 65
Margaret, Princess 48, 50
Maria (Garbo's aunt) 156
Marie Walewska 98-99, 123, 133
Marshall, Herbert 141
Masked Woman, The 146
Maslow, Abraham 13-15, 19, 45, 85, 115, 118
Mason, James 58
Mason, Pamela 58
Mata Hari 24, 27, 100, 107-109, 119, 124, 166, 170
Maxwell, Elsa 64, 155
Mayer, Irene 54, 169
Mayer, Louis B. 25, 33, 46, 53-54, 77, 102-103, 145, 151, 157, 163-69
Mårtensen, Mona 43, 100
McCrea, Joel 148-49
Montgomery, Robert 69
Moore, Colleen 166
Moreno, Antonio 59
Murnau, F.W. 73-74, 172
Mysterious Lady, The 12

N
Nagel, Conrad 12
När Rosorna Slå Ut 80
Negri, Pola 95, 136
New York Nights, 167
Niblo, Fred 59, 164
Nilsson, Ivar 49

Ninotchka 22, 26, 36, 45, 96, 108, 112, 132
Novarro, Ramon 24, 107

O
Odalisque From Smolna, The 35, 140
Olcott, Henry Steele 125
Onassis, Aristotle 21-22, 74, 86, 95, 101
Oswald, Marianne 43, 100
Owen, Catherine Dale 168-69

P
Painted Veil, The 76, 126, 141
Palmborg, Rilla Page 84, 155
Paris, Barry 34, 55
Parkinson, Michael 12
Parsons, Harriet 152
Parsons, Louella 152, 172
Petschler, Erik 156-57
Pickford, Mary 103
Pirandello, Luigi 85
Pollack, Mimi 100
Pope-Hennessy, James 129
Porter, Allen 35

Q
Queen Christina 21, 33, 43-44, 46, 49, 57, 97-98, 109, 119, 135, 148-49, 159
Queen of England 50

R
Randolf, Anders 37
Reinhardt, Max 65
Reisch, Walter 158

Reisfield, Gray 93
Renoir, Auguste 96
Reud, Robert 157
Rée, Max 164
Ring, Ragnar 55, 67
Robertson, John S. 43
Robinson, Edward G. 108
Robson, May 86
Rogers, James 38
Romance 74, 107, 117, 148, 165
Rothschild, Cécile de 74, 96
Rothschild, Élie de 34
Rukeyser, Muriel 100
Russell, Bertrand 131
Ryman, Tyra 156

S
Sabatini, Rafael 66
Sand, George 102
Schenk, Nicholas 54
Scheuer, Phil 165
Schlee, George 33, 74-75, 128
Schlee, Valentina 33, 128
Schmeling, Max 46
Schmiterlow, Vera 73, 100
Schoenberg, Arnold 65
Scott, Zachary 107
Semitjov, Vladimir 35
Seyffertitz, Gustav von 25
Shaw, George Bernard 116
Shayne, Tamara 45
Sherwood, Robert E. 59, 158
Sibelius 25
Silvia, queen of Sweden 79
Single Standard, The 31, 43, 112, 159

Sorensen, Wilhelm 93, 150
Stein, Gertrude 102
Stephenson, William 47-48, 150
Stiller, Mauritz 11-13, 19, 32, 35-36, 53-55, 65, 73, 102, 111, 123, 140, 145, 157, 163-64, 170-71
Stokowski, Leopold 87-88, 125-26
Stone, Lewis 117, 141
Streetcar Named Desire, A 20
Sundborg, Åke 155
Susan Lenox Her Fall and Rise 44, 96, 101, 141
Svenson, Julia 85
Swanson, Gloria 33

T
Talmadge, Norma 167
Taylor, Robert 46
Tchelitchew, Pavel 110
Temptress, The 59, 64, 103, 163, 166
Thalberg, Irving 43, 97, 163-64
Tibbett, Lawrence 118
Torrent 24, 54, 66, 136, 148, 171
Tugboat Annie 77
Two-Faced Woman 24, 26, 67, 76, 84, 99, 102, 109, 156, 172
Tynan, Kenneth 73, 117, 159

V
Vidor, King 168
Viertel, Salka 37, 43, 46-47, 56, 58, 65, 73-74, 96, 98, 102, 131, 133, 137-38, 140, 171-72

Voight, Hubert 26, 43, 118

W
*Wachtmeister, Hörke 35, 63,
68, 75, 131, 138*
Wachtmeister, Nils 63, 75
Watson, Lyall 171
Watts, Richard 170
Wedekind, Kadidja 101
Welles, Orson 12-13, 19
Wenner-Gren, Axel 150
Whitehall, Richard 159
Whitehead, Alfred North 116
Wilber, Ken 139
Wild Orchids 31, 141, 145
Wilder, Billy 25, 158
Williams, Tennessee 20
Williams, Mona Harrison 69
Wilson, Carey 65
Wilson, Colin 115-19, 160
*Woman of Affairs, A 23-24,
97, 99, 101*
Woodridge, Dorothy 12

Y
Young, Roland 67, 76

Moon Laramie is an esoteric author and a Theosophist. He is interested in exploring the power of thought forms, the relationship between the physical and astral worlds, reincarnation and karmic law.

Moon Laramie is the author of The Zombie Inside, A Practical Guide to the Law of Attraction.

He has written for a number of publications including Kindred Spirit and The Best You, and is a regular contributor to The Magic Happens magazine.

www.moonlaramie.com